Bible Fun Stuff

FOR TWEENS

Game-a-thon

David C Cook

transforming lives together

GAME-A-THON
Published by David C. Cook
4050 Lee Vance View
Colorado Springs, CO 80918 U.S.A.

David C. Cook Distribution Canada
55 Woodslee Avenue, Paris, Ontario, Canada N3L 3E5

David C. Cook U.K., Kingsway Communications
Eastbourne, East Sussex BN23 6NT, England

David C. Cook and the graphic circle C logo
are registered trademarks of Cook Communications Ministries.

Cover Design by BMB Design
Cover Photography © Brad Armstrong Photography
Interior Design by Rebekah Lyon
Illustrations by Hector Adrian Borlasca

ISBN 978-1-4347-6857-5

Printed in United States
First Printing 2008

1 2 3 4 5 6 7 8 9 10

FOR TWEENS

Game-a-thon

Table of Contents

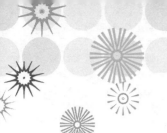

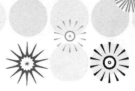

The Lowdown on *Game-a-thon*

If you lead tween kids, *Game-a-thon*, a resource jam-packed with wild and crazy games that teach God's Word to upper elementary kids, is for you. Tweens are social and energetic; they seek attention and crave excitement. *Game-a-thon* games will get them moving, excited, and thrilled to learn and to be with each other. Not only are these games fun and educational, but they provide a format for tweens to learn, problem solve, encourage each other, and work together as a team.

Game-a-thon is packed full of 26 games in an easy-to-follow format. Each game is biblically grounded with Scripture and correlates with David C. Cook's *Bible-in-Life* or *Echoes* Sunday school curriculum. Or you can use the **Scripture** or **Topic Index** in the back of the book to tie in with any other curriculum or issue you on which you want to focus. The **Bible Background** supplies further information about the Scripture reference. **Teacher Tips** offers suggestions on how to raise the level of play or what to watch for when playing the game.

Each game also offers the following:

Gear List: The materials needed for the game. We have kept in mind materials that are easily accessible and quickly gathered for your convenience.

Pre-Game Warm-Up: This includes brief instructions on how to set up the playing area or additional materials that might need to be prepared beforehand.

Game Over: The game ends with debriefing questions to help analyze the meaning of the game and tie it together with application to the Bible and their lives.

The games in this book help kids connect with Bible truths and carry God's Word with them as they leave the classroom. Here are a few suggestions for keeping the fun in classroom games.

- There's nothing as boring as a ten-minute explanation of game rules. Keep rules as simple as possible and think through your explanation in advance so you can present it quickly.
- Be sensitive to differing ability levels. If you think that the skills necessary for a certain game might leave some out, adapt it to include everyone. Extend time limits, shorten distance requirements, play in pairs, and so on.
- Allow enough time for a game so kids feel they've been able to enjoy it without rushing, especially if it's a task that may take a few attempts to master.
- It's a good idea to stop a game while tweens are still enjoying it—before they've gotten tired of it. Tell them when the last round begins, so the end doesn't take them by surprise.
- Think through ahead of time. Anticipate how much noise a game makes and whether it's appropriate for your setting. Do you have enough space? Enough helpers?

So ignite your tweens and let the games begin as you help them move further along in their relationships with God!

Sheep Sharing

Scripture:
Genesis 13

Memory Verse:
If it is possible,
as far as it depends on you,
live at peace with everyone.
Romans 12:18

Bible Background

Ur of the Chaldeans (kal-DEE-uns) was probably located in what is now southern Iraq. Abram, a descendant of Noah's son Shem, lived there with his family, and there he married Sarai. Abram's family, led by his father, Terah, migrated to a place called Haran. Both Ur and Haran were centers of worship of the moon-god. (Haran was also the name of one of Abram's brothers—the father of Lot—but is not the same word in the original language. Abram and Sarai took their nephew in after Haran's death.)

Even before Abram left Ur, God had called him out of Haran (see Acts 7:2), and he followed God's instructions to move to Canaan, accompanied by Lot. After Abram arrived in Canaan, the Lord promised him that his descendants would inherit the land.

As Abram and Lot became increasingly wealthy in flocks and herds, a shortage of good pastureland led to disputes among their herdsmen. To avoid trouble, Abram offered Lot his choice of land: either the fertile, well-watered lowlands of the Jordan River valley or the rough highlands of Canaan.

When given the choice, Lot chose the Jordan valley and settled near Sodom, an area notorious for wickedness. Abram chose the high road of yielding in a quarrelsome situation. While it may have looked like Lot got the better end of the deal, God's promises to Abram were still to be fulfilled.

Sometimes we may question the effort required to get along with difficult people in our lives. But God wants us to make every effort to get along with others—even to go out of our way to make peace. "If it is possible, as far as it depends on you, live at peace with everyone" (Rom. 12:18).

Teacher Tips

- You might like to play some lively music during the game.

- Use enough "sheep" so that each player will have to make multiple trips to the fold to gather all the sheep.

- This game can be a little messy. Ask kids to help you clean up after playing, before you sit down to debrief.

Pre-Game Warm-Up

- Assign players to two groups, the Abraham group and the Lot group. Leave the kids mixed together in one large group, but make sure they know which teams they're on.

- Point out that each group has a basket. Place the baskets a little apart from each other on one side of the room. Make sure each group knows which basket is theirs.

- Give each child a spatula or serving spoon.

- Dump a large amount of cotton balls, popcorn, or packing peanuts at the opposite side of the room from the baskets.

Gear List

- Cotton balls, popcorn, or packing peanuts

- Spatulas or serving spoons, one for each tween

- Baskets or buckets

Let's Play!

We're going to get out in the field with Abraham and Lot and figure out how to share the land for our sheep!

When I give the signal, use the spatulas or serving spoons to scoop up "sheep" and tenderly carry them to the shepherds' folds (baskets). **Make sure you don't drop any sheep! They won't like that. But you can't touch the sheep with your hands.**

Give the signal for play to begin. You can play for a designated amount of time, or until all of the sheep in the center have been carried to the baskets.

Game Over

Debrief the game activities with the following discussion.

God had blessed Abraham and his nephew with lots of sheep! They had to figure out a way to share the land the sheep grazed on and the water they drank. Abraham did everything he could to get along with Lot.

- **Tell about a time when you didn't get along with one of your friends or someone in your family.** *(Answers will vary.)* Be willing to share such a time from your own life if no one volunteers.

- **What do you think is the hardest part of trying to get along with other people?** *(being nice when no one else is, not arguing, sharing, etc.)*

- **Name three things you can do to get along better with other people.** *(be nice, be polite, be willing to share, take turns, be generous, etc.)*

Faith Targets

Scripture:
Exodus 11—12; 29:15-18;
John 1:29

Memory Verse:
In him we have redemption through his blood, the forgiveness of sins, in accordance with the riches of God's grace.
Ephesians 1:7

Bible Background

To understand the unfolding of God's plan of redemption, we need an overview of biblical history. When Pharaoh refused to release the enslaved Hebrews, God brought ten plagues upon Egypt. The final plague brought death to all the firstborn sons of the Egyptians, as well as the firstborn of their cattle.

God, however, delivered His people from death as they followed the instructions He gave Moses. Each household killed a year-old male lamb and sprinkled its blood on the sides and top of the doorway. The blood indicated that a sacrifice had been offered as a substitute.

In time the killing of the Passover lamb became a picture of redemption from sin (1 Cor. 5:7). The sacrificed lamb taking away an Israelite's sin is a picture of the Messiah, the Lamb of God, dying in the place of sinners (Isa. 53:4-7). Up until Christ's death God's people depended on the sacrifice of a lamb to receive forgiveness. After Christ's death, people were able to enter a right relationship with God by accepting the once-for-all sacrifice of His Son, Jesus, on the cross.

The concept of God's grace—receiving something freely offered, something we don't deserve—is a humbling process. Do you sometimes think you have to "earn" God's grace in some way? The truth is, you can't. The grace offered is already paid in full by Jesus. How can you rest in God's grace more securely today?

Teacher Tips

- If you have class time available, you can have kids assemble the set of targets.

- If you'd like to send the game home with each student, collect enough supplies for each student to make a set of targets.

- Adjust the distance between the tossing line and the target according to the ability of your students. Mark several lines and let kids choose which line they want to use. Help players understand that some kids may need to be a little closer to succeed. If a player chooses the closest line and scores well, that player should move back on his or her next turn.

Pre-Game Warm-Up

- Ahead of time, assemble a set of targets. Cut the largest circle possible from one color of a felt square. Then cut out three more circles from the other colors of felt so that each one is smaller than the one before. Glue the largest circle to one half of the cardboard. Glue the other circles on top of the largest one in a stack. Then use the marker to print these words and point values along the outer edges of the circles:

  Jesus 50   (smallest circle)
  Love   25   (second circle)
  Hope   10   (third circle)
  Faith   5   (largest circle)

- Now create the balls that players will toss at the target. Cut a strip of hook and loop strips into pieces that will wrap around the circumference of a large pom-pom. Use the side that has the "hooks" and attach one piece to a pom-pom. The other side will stick to felt. Make several pom-poms to toss.

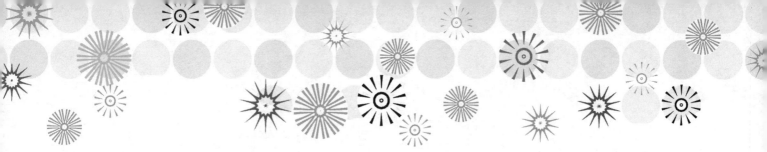

Gear List

- Sheets of cardboard
- 4 colors of large felt squares
- Fabric or permanent markers
- Strips of self-sticking hook and loop fasteners
- Large pom-poms of various colors
- Glue
- Scissors
- Paper and pencil

Let's Play!

Because Jesus takes the place of the Old Testament sacrifices, we have love, hope, and faith in our lives. We have a relationship with God! Let's celebrate by taking careful aim to know God better. Our aim should be to have faith, hope, and love direct us more to Jesus and to have the courage to share about Him with others.

For play, prop the target up against a wall. Position the half of the cardboard that has the target at the top. You can play on the floor or a tabletop. Players toss the pom-poms at the felt target and see if they can make them stick. Let each player toss three pom-poms in each round. Use the paper and pencil to keep score. Score only the pom-poms that stick.

Game Over

Debrief the game activity with the following discussion. Remember there are no right or wrong answers to some questions, but use them instead to open discussions with your kids.

Because of Jesus' sacrifice for us, we can know God and live with Him forever. God loves us, and our faith in Him gives us hope every day of our lives.

- **When you think about the sacrifice that Jesus made for you, how do you feel?** *(grateful, humble, uncomfortable, etc.)*

- **Why are faith, hope, and love good targets to have in our lives?** *(because they help us, they're gifts, they're fruits of the Spirit, etc.)*

- **How could you use a game like this one to tell friends about Jesus?** *(I could ask them to play and then share about why these are good things to aim for in life.)*

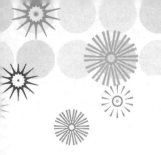

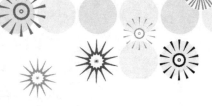

Prayer Catchers

Scripture:
1 Samuel 1:1—2:21

Memory Verse:
The LORD is close to the brokenhearted and saves those who are crushed in spirit.
Psalm 34:18

Bible Background

Hannah lived in Canaan during the time when judges ruled the Hebrew people. Elkanah, Hannah's husband, had two wives: Peninnah and Hannah. Polygamy was practiced even by godly men in ancient times, although it was never God's original intent. Peninnah had children while Hannah had none. This was the source of Hannah's deep grief. In Bible times a woman's whole life was her family, and to have no children was a heartbreaking situation.

Three times a year every Israelite male was required to appear before the Lord at the central sanctuary. Elkanah would have traveled to Shiloh, about a 15-mile journey (1 Sam. 1:3). The festival referred to in verse 3 was probably the Feast of Tabernacles that not only commemorated God's care for His people during the desert journey to Canaan, but more especially celebrated God's blessing on the year's crops. On such a joyous occasion, Hannah may have felt the intensity of her own barrenness even more.

Hannah's prayer is often referred to as the "Magnificat of the Old Testament" because it's similar to Mary's song (Luke 1:46-55). The great source of joy in Hannah's prayer isn't simply in the baby she now had, but it was also in the God who had heard the prayer of her broken heart.

Hannah poured out her soul to God in the anguish of her unfulfilled dreams. She believed that the Lord would hear the prayer of a broken heart. Is your heart broken or hurting today? Are you able to trust God for now, knowing that there will come a time to rejoice again?

Teacher Tips

- If you have more kids than can play at once in the space you have, rotate the catcher job by having groups of four kids with one towel play at a time. After they catch an item, they move to the side and make room for another group of four. If you have more space, have three or four groups with towels playing.

- Have kids lob paper wads. But before wadding up the paper, have kids write personal prayers on them.

- If the task seems too easy, have kids play on their knees. This makes it a little harder to throw and harder to move as a group with a towel to catch objects.

Pre-Game Warm-Up

- Set up the temple wall to divide the game area. Make it taller than the kids' heads so they can't see over it, but can still throw over it.

Gear List

- Something to serve as a "temple wall" (large screen, blanket draped over a rope, plywood board securely propped up, stacked boxes, etc.)

- Soft lobbing objects (paper wads, foam balls, small beanbags, etc.) in buckets or boxes

- Towels or small blankets

Let's Play!

Hannah went to the house of the Lord to pray. She prayed and prayed and prayed for the Lord to give her a child. God was listening! Every time Hannah tossed up a prayer, God was there to catch it. This game reminds us that God catches every prayer we toss His way.

Assign kids to two groups and position one group on each side of the "temple wall." Give one group the buckets of lobbing objects. Give the other group the catching objects (towels and blankets). One group lobs objects over the wall. Emphasize using underhand throws—no hard throwing! They can't see where they are throwing. The group on the other side can't see where the objects might come, but it's their job to catch them with towels or blankets. Demonstrate how several kids can hold the edges of one towel and move at the same time to catch an object with it. Let them practice catching a few balls that they can see coming.

Have no more than two to three lobbers throwing for each group holding a blanket. Set the buckets of objects at the back of the game area, and instruct the lobbers to run to the bucket, remove only one object at a time, run to the temple wall to gently lob it over, and then run back for another item.

You may set a certain amount of time or you may play until all the objects have been lobbed. Items caught in the towels can be tossed to one side. Those missed are left on the ground. When finished, have the kids collect the items they caught and count them. The team that caught the most wins. Then the kids can change sides to play again.

Game Over

Debrief the game activity.

Sometimes when we pray, it might feel like no one is listening. Hannah may have felt this way as she waited for God to give her a child. Just like we couldn't see over the wall to throw our prayers, we don't always understand what God is planning to do. But we can be sure He'll always "catch" our prayers.

■ **What might make you think that God isn't catching your prayers?** *(can't see the answer, things don't seem to change, etc.)*

■ **What can help you keep on throwing your prayers to God?** *(write them down in a journal along with answers, talk and pray with others, believe His promises, etc.)*

■ **Share something you would like other people to pray for along with you.** If kids are too shy to share, open this time by sharing something from your own life. You may close the time by praying about these things together.

Where, Oh Where, Has the New King Gone?

Scripture:
1 Samuel 8—10

Memory Verse:
Show me your ways, O LORD,
teach me your paths.
Psalm 25:4

Bible Background

Samuel had faithfully followed God in his leading of Israel for many years, ever since his childhood. But now Israel wanted a king. The Israelites' request came around 400 years after they entered the promised land. Their reasons: Samuel was old, his sons were dishonest, and Israel wanted to be like other nations, with a king who would lead them in battle against their enemies.

When Saul approached Samuel, it was because he thought the prophet would be able to tell him where he could find his father's lost donkeys. Samuel not only knew where the donkeys were, but also knew that Saul was the one God had chosen as king. The next day Samuel took Saul to the edge of town and anointed him king. When Samuel first told him that he was the "desire" of Israel (a reference to Israel's desire for a king), Saul protested. He had no ambitions of being king. His humility was a good thing.

Israel's desire for a king came from that familiar cry, "But everyone else is doing it!" At times we all seem to have that desire to be like the people around us. If the people around us are attempting to follow God's ways, then that desire isn't necessarily a bad thing. But what if what everyone else is doing is contrary to God's ways? When do you feel the most pressure to follow the "popular way" instead?

Teacher Tips

- If you're concerned that some of your kids might get too rambunctious, use large foam balls instead of soccer balls.

- If you don't have plastic cones, you can use other items for game markers. For instance, fill gallon-size jugs or two-liter bottles with sand so they'll stay in place.

- Depending on the size of your group and the temperament of your players, you may want to make this activity less competitive. Have players take turns navigating the cones, but don't emphasize speed or winning. You might use only one set of cones to discourage comparison and competition between teams.

Pre-Game Warm-Up

- Set up six or eight cones in a line, spaced evenly about two or three feet apart. Make a line of cones for each six or eight players.

- Assign players to teams. Each team should have six to eight players. Try to keep the teams as even as possible in number and ability. Have each team line up behind a line of cones.

Gear List

- Plastic cones or sand-filled plastic bottles

- Soccer balls or large foam balls

Let's Play!

Saul was wandering around looking for his lost donkeys. Imagine you're zig-zagging around the hillsides of Judea looking for donkey tracks. The first part of this game is to dribble the ball between your feet and zig-zag between the cones. Demonstrate or ask a volunteer to help you demonstrate. **If you lose control of the ball and it rolls away, you can pick it up and bring it back. But you have to start at the last cone that you passed.**

After Saul met Samuel and found out he was going to be king, he wasn't sure he wanted the job! He was a head taller than the rest of the people, so he was keeping his head down and hiding among the supplies. After you dribble the ball around the last cone, go into Saul's hiding position. Get down on all fours and keep your head down. Use your head to push the ball back through the cones. Demonstrate or ask a volunteer to demonstrate. **Then pass the ball on to the next player on your team.**

If you have a team with one less player than other teams, one player can take two turns. Play until all teams have finished. If you've chosen a non-competitive option, wait for everyone to have a turn. Encourage kids waiting their turn to cheer on the ones dribbling or pushing the ball with their heads.

Game Over

Debrief the game activity.

Israel wanted a king because they wanted to be like everyone else. God gave them the king they asked for, but it wasn't really what He wanted for His people. At times you may want to be like everyone else too, but God may be calling you to do something different. Remember He will also give you the courage to do things His way.

- **What makes us want to do things to be popular or like everyone else?** *(We want to fit in. We want to be liked. We want to do what our friends are doing, etc.)*

- **What if the popular way isn't God's way? How do we figure out what to do?** *(pray, ask other believers, read God's Word, etc.)*

- **Name a situation where it's better to do something God's way instead of the popular way.** *(Answers will vary.)* Be prepared to share an example from your own life as well.

Battle-Line Stomp

Scripture:
1 Samuel 17

Memory Verse:
The LORD is my light and my salvation—whom shall I fear? The LORD is the stronghold of my life—of whom shall I be afraid?
Psalm 27:1

Bible Background

Goliath may have been just three inches shy of bumping his head on a basketball hoop—without stretching! At nine feet, nine inches tall, he would have stood two feet, three inches taller than the famous professional basketball player Yao Ming. Goliath's spear weighed over 30 pounds, the weight of two bowling balls! No wonder the Israelites—who were probably shorter than an average American adult—were frightened by Goliath!

Scripture calls Goliath a champion. This practice of using individual champions, instead of a whole army, to fight was used by the ancient Greeks. The Philistines may have been remotely related to the Greeks.

Goliath's taunts were not only a reproach to Israel's army, but an insult to their God as well. Because David was so confident that God was able to defeat even the mighty Goliath (vs. 37), he couldn't understand the Israelites' fear. He was dumbfounded that none of them had stood up for the name of the Lord.

David faced a huge, daunting giant, seemingly without fear. How did he do it? We all function without fear at times. We may cower before the "giants" in life that taunt and challenge us. But we can remember David and where he got his confidence and strength. They are available to us today, if we but ask.

Teacher Tips

- You may want to arrange to have assistants available. Not all kids will be steady on the stilts in this activity. Assistants can walk alongside them and spot them if they become unsteady.

- You can make this a competitive relay game between teams or a simple activity that lets kids try a challenge.

- Use a hammer and nail to make holes in the sides of coffee cans.

Pre-Game Warm-Up

- In advance: Make coffee can stilts. Plan on at least two pairs. If you have a lot of kids and think you might need more than two teams, you might want to have more. Turn coffee cans upside down, so the open end is on the ground. Use a hammer and a nail to punch a hole in each side of the closed bottom end of each can. Cut two four-foot lengths of string for each pair of stilts. Slip one end of the string through each hole. Tie off the ends inside the cans to create loops.

- Use masking tape to mark off two starting lines facing each other, about 15 feet apart. If your students turn out to be adept at walking on stilts and your space permits, move the starting lines further apart. In the center, use tape to mark a battle line.

Gear List

- Large empty coffee cans, one pair per team
- Hammer and nail
- Heavy twine or string
- Masking tape

Let's Play!

Line up the kids in two teams behind the start lines.

We usually look at this Bible story from the point of view of David. Have you ever wondered what it felt like to be Goliath? He thought he was so powerful that nothing could take him down. He found out the truth that day when David pulled out his slingshot. We're going to take turns being Goliath stomping out to the battle line. Of course, to do that, we have to be tall! That's why we have stilts. We're going to find out that being big and powerful isn't as easy as it looks. Demonstrate how to stand on the cans and pull on the string loops to keep your feet on the cans.

One player from each team will stomp out to the center—the battle line—then turn around and return to the start line. Play until everyone has had a turn. Remind kids to cheer each other on.

Game Over

Debrief the game activity.

David was a shepherd boy with no armor. King Saul tried to give David his armor, but it didn't fit. Besides, David didn't want it. He knew armor wasn't going to make the difference that day. He knew that the deliverance needed would come through God alone.

- **Why was David so sure he was going to win the battle against Goliath?** *(He knew that God was the one fighting the battle for him, and no one could defeat God.)*

- **How can this story help you when you get into a situation that seems like you can't win?** *(It can remind me to trust God and rely on His strength.)*

- **Why is it important to remember where our help really comes from?** *(because our strength fails at times, because only God will never fail, etc.)*

Friends, Friends Everywhere

Scripture:
1 Samuel 20

Memory Verse:
For we are God's workmanship, created in Christ Jesus to do good works, which God prepared in advance for us to do.
Ephesians 2:10

Bible Background

The story of David and Jonathan presents one of the most endearing scriptural accounts of friendship. So loyal was Jonathan to David that he was willing to give up any expectations of inheriting the kingdom of Israel from Saul. It was very difficult for both Jonathan and David to accept the fact that Jonathan's father, Saul, wanted to kill David, but they couldn't escape the facts. David asked Jonathan to discover Saul's true feelings for him, and the two friends developed a plan. David and Jonathan's unusual plan was devised to let David know if any hope of reconciliation existed with Saul.

Jonathan knew that David would be the next king. This is indicated by Jonathan's request that when all of David's enemies (including Saul) were conquered, David would not withdraw his kindness from Jonathan or his family. The Hebrew word translated "kindness" here *(hesed)* was used 250 times in the Old Testament signifying steadfast, unfailing love. *Hesed* [pronounced KEH-sed] was the word used to describe God's faithful love for His people.

David and Jonathan really knew what it meant to be the kind of friends who wanted the best for each other, even at great cost to themselves. A true friend is certainly a gift to be cherished. Help your students learn to be true friends who want the best for each other.

Teacher Tips

- Instead of preparing game cards ahead of time, have kids brainstorm the categories of people and relationships to write on the game cards.

- If you think kids might need some incentive to be creative in ways to express kindness, offer the reward of a piece of wrapped candy or other small treat for each idea they come up with. Encourage them not to repeat what someone has already said.

- If you have a large class, you might want to have two game circles going at the same time.

Pre-Game Warm-Up

- Ahead of time, use markers and construction paper to prepare game cards. In bold lettering, spell out on each sheet a type of person or relationship: classmate, friend, little lost child, neighbor, teammate, kid on the playground, elderly person, teacher, parents, needy family, and so on.

Gear List

- Small, hand-sized beanbags
- Construction paper
- Markers
- Masking tape
- Optional: bag of small treats

Let's Play!

The story of David and Jonathan reminds us that friends want what's best for each other. David knew he had to literally run for his life. He wanted Jonathan's help to figure out what was best. Jonathan, David's friend, showed great kindness to him.

This game gives you a chance to think up ways to treat others with kindness. We all have people in our lives who would like us to say a kind word or do something thoughtful for them.

Flip through the construction paper signs. Have the kids read off the categories. Depending on the size of your group, you may want them to brainstorm some more signs.

- **Where might we run into some of these people?** *(school, neighborhood, shopping malls, etc.)*

- **How many people do you think you see in a day?** *(Answers will vary.)*

Lay the construction paper sheets randomly in a central part of the play area. Have kids arrange themselves in a circle around the papers. Have everyone step back so the circle is at least six feet back from the papers. If necessary, use masking tape to mark lines and remind kids to stay behind the lines.

Have kids take turns tossing a beanbag onto one of the sheets. Ask each player to read the words on the paper the beanbag lands on. Then challenge the player to name a realistic way he or she could express kindness to such a person on an ordinary day. Play until everyone has had a turn. Challenge kids to be genuine in their answers, rather than repeat someone else's answer or say something vague.

Game Over

Debrief the game activity.

Jonathan knew David was in trouble and went out of his way to help him. He didn't do the easiest thing. He did the thing that was best for his friend.

- **How did Jonathan do what was best for David?** *(Jonathan found out the truth that Saul wanted to kill David. He helped David get away and gave him special gifts.)*

- **How does doing what's best for someone else sometimes mean that you have to give up something?** *(Sometimes you let the friend have the last seat or piece of candy, etc.)*

- **What's the hardest part about doing what's best for someone else?** *(not thinking about myself, having to sacrifice, etc.)* **What's the easiest part?** *(the good feelings I get, how it makes them feel, knowing I am pleasing God, etc.)*

Share and Share Alike

Scripture:
1 Samuel 30:1-25

Memory Verse:
And do not forget to do good
and to share with others,
for with such sacrifices
God is pleased.
Hebrews 13:16

Bible Background

Still fleeing from King Saul, David and his men (and their families) had moved into a Philistine area and pretended to be loyal to Achish [A-kish], a Philistine king. This put David in the awkward position of being expected to fight against his own people. At the same time, the Philistine commanders feared that David and his men would turn against them in battle.

Achish expressed confidence in David, who was willing to stay and fight for the Philistines. But God saved David from the sin of fighting his own people when He put it in Achish's heart to send David and his men away from the impending battle with Israel.

When David and his men arrived at the home base of Ziklag, they found it plundered and their families gone. Interestingly, the captors were the Amalekites, whom Saul had been instructed to destroy earlier but failed to do so.

With divine approval, David and his men pursued and defeated the Amalekites, and recovered their families and possessions. David insisted that the spoils be shared with both those who did the fighting and those who had stayed behind because they were too tired to fight. David's sense of fairness wasn't only a display of political savvy, it was a manifestation of godly character. His gestures even went beyond being fair; he showed generosity and mercy.

The concept of fairness is one that tweens are acutely aware of. And one that adults relate to as well. But how difficult is it for your kids to be the ones extending fairness? How often do your own dealings model not only fairness, but mercy and generosity?

Teacher Tips

- Small funnels, instead of lunch bags, will make the task harder, adding to the challenge and fun.

- Adjust the distance between the two groups, depending on how successful kids are at throwing peanuts into the funnels. If it's a hard task, move the lines closer. If they seem to be succeeding easily, move the lines further apart.

- Decide ahead of time how long to play the game. One-third of the way through that time, call a time out and have kids change roles. Two-thirds of the way through the play time, shift roles again.

Pre-Game Warm-Up

- None needed.

Gear List
- Packing peanuts
- Paper lunch bags or small funnels

Let's Play!

When David led the charge to get back what had been stolen from his men, some of the men were too tired to fight. David allowed 200 men to stay behind while he took 400 men with him. They got back everything that had been stolen. The men who fought didn't want to share with the men who had stayed behind. They wanted to keep the loot for themselves. David insisted that they share evenly. Real sharing reflects God's heart of giving even when it doesn't seem fair.

Explain that kids will have a chance to play a game that lets them practice sharing. Assign kids to two groups. Make one group only half as big as the other group. (Two-thirds of the kids are in the large group, one-third in the small group.) Have the groups stand several feet apart. Give the smaller group lunch bags. Give the larger group an ample supply of packing peanuts.

The group with the packing peanuts are the soldiers who fought with David. The group with the lunch bags are the soldiers who were too tired to go to battle. Have the tired soldiers kneel or squat and hold the lunch bags out in front of them. The large group tosses packing peanuts, and the small group tries to catch them in the bags.

Play for a while, then switch roles. Rotate so that everyone gets a chance to be in the small group trying to catch packing peanuts. After a reasonable amount of time, compare how full everyone's bags are.

Game Over

Debrief the game activity.

   David wanted everyone to have an equal share in the loot they brought back from battle. Sharing was more important that what the people thought was fair.

- **Did you get an equal share of the packing peanuts? How do you feel about your share?** *(Answers will vary.)*

- **Why do you think David wanted to share, even if it wasn't fair?** *(Because he knew that was what God wanted him to do. He knew that every job was important, even staying behind with the possessions while the others fought.)*

- **What sometimes makes it hard to share?** *(I don't think the other person deserves a share. I want to keep things for myself, etc.)*

- **What sometimes makes it easy?** *(knowing it's the right thing to do, knowing that I will make the other person happy, etc.)*

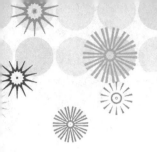

Sneak Attack

Scripture:
2 Samuel 14:25—15:37;
17—18

Memory Verse:
Do not steal. Do not lie.
Do not deceive one another.
Leviticus 19:11

Bible Background

The account of Absalom's rebellion has its roots in David's own sin with Bathsheba. David was warned he would pay a price for his sin. Their son Absalom became part of that price.

First, Absalom murdered an older half-brother who had raped Absalom's sister. Not only was the attack avenged, but this made Absalom the oldest son and, he thought, heir to the throne. When Absalom found out that wasn't the plan, he angrily contrived to get the throne for himself by ingratiating himself to the Israelite people, telling them what they wanted to hear in regard to their complaints against David's government.

When Absalom's popularity increased to the point of having his own army, David fled Jerusalem. This gave the king a chance to rally his own supporters and protect the city from bloodshed. Eventually the two armies clashed.

It's possible that Absalom's abundant hair became caught in the tree limbs as he rode through them, but Scripture only states that his head got caught. Against David's specific orders, Joab, David's general, killed Absalom while Absalom was still stuck in the tree.

The Bible pulls no punches in its description of people who used underhanded means to obtain what they wanted: Jacob comes to mind, and even David in his relationship with Bathsheba. There were clear consequences for this behavior: Jacob ran in fear for his life from his brother Esau, and David and Bathsheba's first child died. As seen in this lesson, Absalom also faced severe consequences for his attempt to sneak the kingdom from his father's grasp.

Clearly, being sneaky isn't something that God will condone. Honesty and integrity in all our dealings is what the Lord desires of us because it reflects who He is in His dealings as well. And God doesn't want us to be drawn in when we're faced with something not fully upright. Romans 12:21 says, "Do not be overcome by evil, but overcome evil with good."

Teacher Tips

- Not all kids can wink. If you think this might be a problem, you can use another gesture that isn't too obvious, such as wrinkling the nose or licking the lips.

- If you have a large group, form more than one circle and play simultaneous rounds.

- If the game seems too easy for your kids, make it more challenging by having more than one enemy and defender. It will be harder to catch more than one person winking.

Pre-Game Warm-Up

- You will need one note card per student. On one card, use the marker to print a "D" and on another card print an "E." The remainder of the cards should be blank.

Gear List

- Note cards, one per student
- Marker

Let's Play!

You might think a king would have an easy life, but that's not always the case. David was king of Israel for 40 years, but some of his sons wanted to have a shot at the job. A lot of spying and deceiving and sneaky stuff went on. David's sons and his officers had to be on their toes at all times, because they could never be sure who they could trust.

Our game today gives us a taste of that life. Who is the enemy? Who will defend you? Who can you trust, and who is being sneaky?

Shuffle and pass out the cards, one per student. Have the kids look at their own cards without revealing who got the "D" and "E" cards. Collect the cards and have kids stand in a circle facing each other. Tell them that the person who got the card with the "E" on it is the "enemy" who will try to make eye contact with others in the circle and "attack" by winking at them without getting caught. Remind the kids: **If you're winked at, quietly sit down. Don't do anything to identify the enemy.**

The person who got the card with the "D" on it is the "defender." This person will try to catch the enemy. The defender watches to try to catch someone winking. The defender calls out the enemy's name whenever he or she knows it.

The object is for the enemy to get everyone out except the defender, or for the defender to stop the attack by correctly identifying the enemy. Encourage everyone to keep looking around the circle at each other. This helps the enemy gain eye contact and keeps the defender vigilant.

The defender gets only two chances, so he or she should not make wild guesses. Two wrong guesses means that the defender is out, and the round is over. If the defender correctly guesses the identity of the enemy, the round is over. Reshuffle the cards and start again.

Game Over

Debrief the game activity.

King David couldn't even trust his own sons! Absalom was sneaking around trying to become king, but that wasn't God's way of doing things.

- **How hard or easy was it to figure out who was the enemy and who was the defender?** *(Answers will vary.)*

- **Describe a situation where you might be tempted to be sneaky to get what you want.** *(when I know I'll get in trouble, when I don't want to share with others, etc.)*

- **Why do you think that being sneaky is not God's way?** *(He wants us to be honest. He wants us to be like Him.)*

Take Aim and Serve

Scripture:
1 Kings 4—10

Memory Verse:
Be sure to fear the LORD
and serve him faithfully
with all your heart;
consider what great things
he has done for you.
1 Samuel 12:24

Bible Background

Peace and prosperity characterized Solomon's reign, and his people lived in security as he ruled over the largest kingdom in Israel's history. Solomon formed alliances with foreign powers, many of them through marriages. His court included government, military, and spiritual leaders, as well as hundreds of servants. It's quite likely that Solomon continually fed and housed several thousand people.

It was through some of these political alliances, particularly the one Solomon had made with Hiram, king of Tyre, that he bartered for building materials for the temple. Even before Solomon's birth, Hiram had provided workmen and timber for the building of David's palace.

The building of the temple was an honor that David had wished for, but was denied (1 Chron. 22:6-10). The temple site was considered holy from the very beginning. All the pounding and rock cutting that required iron tools were done before the materials were brought to the actual building site.

Solomon's service in building the temple for the Lord honored Him. God promises to honor us when we honor Him (1 Sam. 2:30). Sometimes it may seem that your efforts fall short of truly honoring God. But you can ask God to be honored and glorified in your class, through your teaching and in the lives of each one of your students.

Teacher Tips

- Adjust the distance between the start line and the bottles, based on the skill of your students.

- For more of a challenge, use unopened (sealed) water bottles. They'll be harder to knock down.

- Assign a set-up crew who will reset the pins between turns. Make sure the set-up crew gets turns to bowl as well.

Pre-Game Warm-Up

- Ahead of time, write these phrases on the index cards. Tape one card to each bottle.

  ruled with wisdom

  built the temple

  built good relationships

  became famous

  rulers visited him

  had happy officials

  answered hard questions

  always ready to serve

  honored God

  enjoyed God's blessing

Gear List

- 10 empty one-liter plastic bottles
- 10 index cards
- Marker
- Medium-sized rubber ball
- Masking tape

Let's Play!

Arrange the bottles on the floor in a triangle, the way bowling pins are arranged. Use masking tape to mark off a start line about 10 or 15 feet away from the bottles.

Solomon started his rule as a great king. He did a lot of wonderful things for the people, and God rewarded him. Take a few minutes for kids to read the words written on the bottles as a review of the highlights of Solomon's life.

These qualities of Solomon's life are something to admire and imitate. Let's see how many of them we can aim for. Let kids take turns bowling down the bottles. Each player gets two rolls to try to knock down as many pins as possible. If you'd like, keep score. Let everyone bowl the same number of rounds and see what the total scores are.

Game Over

Debrief the game activity.

> **During this time in his life, Solomon honored and served God well.**

- **Name some ways that you can imitate Solomon and the way he served God.** *(help others, serve, share, etc.)*

- **Why is God honored when we serve Him?** *(because it reflects a heart that is like His heart, because He is glorified when we obey and serve, etc.)*

- **How can other people learn more about God by the way we serve Him?** *(We show what God is like. They can learn He is good and loving.)*

Dangerous Quicksand

Scripture:

1 Kings 11—12

Memory Verse:

Teach me your way, O LORD,
and I will walk in your truth;
give me an undivided heart,
that I may fear your name.

Psalm 86:11

Bible Background

Foreign women, a weakness of Solomon's, were partly responsible for his downfall. He had 700 wives and 300 concubines. Many of these women were from idolatrous countries. The marriages were often the product of Solomon's political alliances. Marrying foreign women went against God's prohibitions in Deuteronomy 7:3 and 17:17. But God apparently was willing to allow Solomon to live this way as long as he worshiped only the one true God.

In the 24th year of Solomon's 40-year reign, God appeared to Solomon a second time and warned him not to follow other gods (1 Kings 9:6-7). When Solomon began worshiping his wives' false gods, the Lord was angry. God told Solomon that the kingdom would be divided; however, this would not happen during Solomon's lifetime. What God said to Solomon matched word for word Samuel's statement to King Saul when his disobedience lost the kingdom for his heirs.

The division of the kingdom was tragic. Israel never again reached the level of prosperity it had enjoyed under Solomon's reign. Both parts of the kingdom turned from God, ending up in exile—never to fully return. God left the tribe of Judah to Solomon's heir—a small glimmer of hope that hints at God's unconditional covenant with Solomon's father, David.

The people Solomon surrounded himself with greatly influenced him. The people around us affect us both positively and negatively. That's why God warns us strongly about the company we keep. Help your students see that they need to choose their friends wisely—ones who will strengthen them in their walk with the Lord instead of pulling them away.

Teacher Tips

- If you have a large class, prepare two or more buckets of sand and marbles for simultaneous play.

- Ask one of the kids to assist you by being the timekeeper.

- You can play this game with individual players or pairs of players sifting through the sand together. Or, you can assign kids to teams and keep a cumulative score for each team.

Pre-Game Warm-Up

- Ahead of time, spread a sheet or tablecloth on the floor to help contain the mess.

- Fill the bucket with clean, dry sand. Stir in 50 marbles. Ten marbles should be red, and the rest can be a mixture of colors.

Gear List

- 10 red marbles
- 40 non-red marbles
- Sand
- Bucket
- Sheet or tablecloth
- Stopwatch or watch with second hand

Let's Play!

Solomon started out on the right path when he became king, but then he started sliding down a slippery slope right into a pile of quicksand that swallowed him up. He made some decisions that showed his heart wasn't following God the way it had in the beginning. He didn't choose his relationships carefully.

Imagine you're Solomon and the bucket is full of your decisions and relationships. You don't want to get swallowed by the quicksand. You want to make the right decisions about your relationships.

Explain that each player will have ten seconds to sift through the sand and grab as many marbles as possible. They get one point for every marble they pull out that is not red. They can reach in as many times as they want during the ten seconds. Anyone who grabs a red marble loses the rest of his or her turn. Put all the marbles back in the sand after each turn and mix them in.

Game Over

Debrief the game activity.

Solomon's bad choices had tragic consequences for the whole nation of Israel. After Solomon died, the nation split into two kingdoms. Never again did Israel have the peace and prosperity they enjoyed during Solomon's wiser days. We don't always realize the impact our choices will have down the line.

■ **How difficult was it to know whether you were choosing the right color of marbles?** *(Answers will vary.)*

■ **Why is it hard to make right choices when we can't be sure what will happen?** *(We might be unsure of what way to choose. We might be afraid of making the wrong choice.)*

■ **Name something specific that you can do to help you make better choices in your relationships.** *(pray, ask for input from others, write out possible consequences of each choice, etc.)*

As Close as It Gets

Scripture:
1 Kings 18

Memory Verse:
The LORD is the true God;
he is the living God,
the eternal King.
Jeremiah 10:10

Bible Background

The books 1 and 2 Kings were originally one book that traced the history of the kings of Israel and Judah from the reign of Solomon through the Babylonian captivity. The northern kingdom, Israel, was ruled by kings who rejected God. First Kings 18 recounts the life of the wicked King Ahab.

The first mention of Baal is found in Judges 2:13. Baal was a Canaanite fertility and weather god whose name meant "lord." Baal worship often involved ritual prostitution and sometimes child sacrifices. Elijah was sent by God to put a stop to the Israelites' idol worship. He not only predicted a severe drought, but he told Ahab that only his word would end it. A three-year drought ensued, after which Elijah returned and challenged the king to a contest between God and Baal.

The 450 prophets of Baal prayed, cried, and cut themselves to get an answer, but of course, Baal never answered. Then it was Elijah's turn. He prepared the Lord's altar, dug a trench around it, prepared the sacrifice, and then ordered four large jars of water to be emptied on the altar. Contrast Elijah's simple prayer in 1 Kings 18:36–37 with the frantic prayers of the prophets of Baal. In response, God sent fire that not only consumed the sacrifice but the altar as well.

It was this display of power that convinced the Israelites to follow the one true God after Elijah's "duel" with the prophets of Baal. God's power hasn't diminished between Elijah's time and ours. That same power is available to us today to remind us to keep following the one true God. While you may not have witnessed such an act of power such as the one Elijah witnessed, have you seen or felt the power of God in your own life or the lives of others around you?

Teacher Tips

- The number of kids that can fit in one hoop depends on several variables: the size of the kids, how close they are willing to squish together, and so on. Don't push them beyond their comfort level, but keep the challenge up!

- Have enough hoops on hand so that everyone can play if four or five kids are in a hoop together.

- Kids in a hoop trying to move together can be challenging. Remind them to slow down and move together in order to keep everyone safe.

Pre-Game Warm-Up

- Use masking tape to mark a starting line at one end of the room. Line up the players in several groups behind the starting line and facing the opposite wall.

- Give one hoop to the first player on each team. Have each of those players step into the middle of the hoop and hold it at waist level. Tell the kids that the players in the hoop represent people who are surrounded by the one true God and are choosing to follow Him. Explain that this game symbolizes how others might follow our example if we "capture" their attention by living for God.

Gear List

- Hula hoops, one per group
- Masking tape

Let's Play!

When we choose to follow God, the way Elijah did, other people notice. Then they want to follow God, too. We can help them do that by sticking close together and supporting each other.

The object of the game is to see how many players can fit inside a hoop and move together. The first player should invite the second player to step inside the hoop. Together, they walk to the other end of the room and back. Then they invite a third player to join them inside the hoop. They keep moving back and forth across the room, adding a player to the hoop with each trip. (Let kids decide for themselves how many can fit inside the hoop. As long as new people are completely inside the hoop and the group can keep moving safely, they can keep adding players.)

Explain that after the first people return to their starting lines, the second person in each group should get inside the hoop with the first person and together move the hoop to the opposite wall and back.

Game Over

Debrief the game activity.

Elijah started out as just one person who was following the true God. By the end of the story, he was calling all the people to decide for themselves if they would follow God.

- **Who are some people who show you how to follow God?** *(pastors, parents, teachers, youth leaders, friends, etc.)*

- **How do your actions or words help other people decide to follow God?** *(Actions can show how good God is and how He loves them. Rude or mean behavior can turn people away.)*

- **Describe some situations where you would like to follow God more closely.** *(Answers will vary.)* You should be prepared to share from your own life as well.

Double Whammy

Scripture:
2 Kings 2:1-15

Memory Verse:
The LORD is my strength
and my shield;
my heart trusts in him,
and I am helped.
Psalm 28:7

Bible Background

When it came time for Elijah to be taken up to heaven, Elisha requested that he be made Elijah's heir—to be as good a prophet in Israel as Elijah had been. The "double portion" sounds as if Elisha was expressing the desire to be twice as great as Elijah, but it likely referred to the double portion of an inheritance that a firstborn son received. Because of his persistence in sticking with Elijah, God granted Elisha's request.

The phrase "company of prophets" literally means "sons of prophets." This was an allusion to the prophetic schools that thrived in Elisha's day. These schools first appeared shortly after the people of Israel entered the promised land. God raised up these bands of prophets to encourage and nurture the people spiritually. Nothing more is heard about these schools until the time of Elijah and Elisha. Both of these prophets had a strong ministry in Israel, and they needed the companies of prophets for assistance.

After Elijah was taken up to heaven, Elisha picked up the mantle (Elijah's cloak) that had fallen on the ground. Receiving the mantle meant that Elisha now had the authority that Elijah had, just as Moses' authority passed in succession to Joshua. (See Deut. 34.) Elisha had been mentored by the best—Elijah. But with Elijah's sudden departure, tough changes were ahead as Elisha assumed his new responsibilities without Elijah nearby to help him.

When tough changes come, are you ever tempted to push the panic button or grumble? Both are normal, human responses. Sometimes God allows tough changes in our lives to help us learn to depend on Him. He may also allow them to help us test what we value. Elisha valued serving God well, no matter what changes lay ahead. Consider what you value most about your relationship with God.

Teacher Tips

- If you think your kids will find bathroom tissue inappropriately amusing, you can do this activity with rolls of paper towels instead.

- If time allows, have kids change roles so everyone has a turn to be wrapped and do the wrapping.

- Have the kids plan in advance what qualifies as a great cocoon and judge each other's work according to the standards they set. Some examples might be: no loose ends, snug fitting, no clothing showing, and so on. Go with the ideas that come from the kids.

Pre-Game Warm-Up

- None needed.

Gear List

- Bathroom tissue or paper towel rolls, one for every two students

Let's Play!

Elisha wanted to do something big for God, but knew there would be some tough changes. He wanted to be ready for those challenges. Our game is going to remind us of what it takes to be ready when tough changes are ahead.

Have kids count off, "1," "2," "1," "2," until all are identified as either a 1 or a 2. Pair kids up in 1-2 combinations. If you have an uneven number, ask a teen or adult helper to be a partner.

Tell the kids that "1" is a caterpillar and "2" is going to help "1" spin a cocoon. Give each pair a roll of bathroom tissue. At your signal, "2" wraps "1" completely in bathroom tissue, except for the face. Let kids know you'll give a signal when the wrapping should stop, but don't let them know how much time they have. Let them feel the stress of not knowing and trying to be ready! Remind them that the cocoon should be snug. A caterpillar has to really work to get out of a cocoon.

After a time, call "stop" and admire the cocoons. Afterward, let the kids burst out like butterflies and help clean up the mess!

Game Over

Debrief the game activity.

When Elisha took over Elijah's ministry, he had to be ready for big changes in his life just like a caterpillar transforming into a butterfly.

- **Why does a caterpillar spin a cocoon?** *(to transform from a caterpillar to a butterfly)*

- **The cocoon is the caterpillar's shelter while it is changing into a butterfly. What would happen if the butterfly stayed in the shelter of the cocoon even after it was done changing?** *(it wouldn't fit, it would die, it would get sick, etc.)*

Unless the butterfly leaves its cocoon, it will never be able to fly and do what it was created to do. In fact, if you help a butterfly in any way to break out of its cocoon, it will not be strong enough to survive.

- **What are some things in your life that you have to be strong for? Share them if you feel comfortable doing so.** *(Answers will vary.)* Be prepared to share a circumstance from your own life.

Remember, when we face tough changes, God is there with His power.

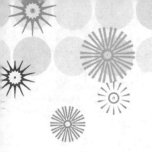

Keep On Moving

Scripture:
Ezra 1—6

Memory Verse:
I lift up my eyes to the hills—
where does my help come from?
My help comes from the LORD,
the Maker of heaven and earth.
Psalm 121:1-2

Bible Background

When Cyrus, the Persian king, took control of
Babylon, he issued a decree permitting the Jews to
return to Jerusalem. The Jews took along many
things, including the gold and silver temple vessels.

The first priority was the restoration of temple worship. After the great altar was built, the
Feast of Tabernacles was celebrated and worship of the Lord was formally restored.

During the second year, the foundation of the temple was laid and the Jews had a great
worship service. The joyful shouts of the worshipers were almost drowned out by the sorrowful
cries of the elderly who remembered the beauty of the old temple.

The Samaritans came and wanted to help. But they were not welcomed to assist with the
temple rebuilding, and so they began hindering that work. The Samaritans sent complaint letters
to several rulers of Persia about the rebuilding of Jerusalem. Finally, an official order came to stop
construction.

When the prophets Haggai (HAG-ee-eye) and Zechariah encouraged the Jews to go on
building, Zerubbabel resumed work. He sent word to the Persian king that Cyrus had authorized
the work. King Darius found the record of Cyrus's decree and sent word to continue work on the
temple. After nearly 17 years, work on the temple was finally resumed and completed. With great
joy the people dedicated the new building.

During the rebuilding of the temple, the Jews got very discouraged as they met numerous
long delays. We can get discouraged as well when things just don't seem to go right. But the Jews
were encouraged and trusted God because He was in control. No matter how chaotic or troubled
the world or our personal lives become, God is in control now, too.

Teacher Tips

- Instead of preparing the cones ahead of time, let kids help you set up the game.

- You may want to let kids (especially those with breathing problems) play in pairs to avoid getting dizzy. They could take turns blowing or blow together to make the foil cone move more quickly.

- An alternative to having kids hold the string is to secure it to objects in your room. Make sure it's at an appropriate height for the kids to blow the cones along the string.

Pre-Game Warm-Up

- Ahead of time, cut circles out of aluminum foil. Make each circle about eight inches in diameter. Then make one cut in from the edge to the center of the circle. Pull the cut edges so they overlap and the foil forms a cone. Leave enough of a hole at the peak of the cone to thread string through later. Seal the seam with tape. Make enough foil cones so that every player will have one.

- Next, cut heavy string into lengths of four yards. Thread the cones onto a piece of heavy string through the small hole at the top of the cone.

Gear List

- Aluminum foil
- Scissors
- Transparent tape
- Heavy string

Let's Play!

When God's people went back to Jerusalem, they carried with them some gold and silver objects that belonged in the temple. In this game, we'll help get the silver temple objects back where they belong. We'll blow them from Persia to Jerusalem!

For each string of cones, ask two kids to hold the string between them. Emphasize that they must hold it taut. You can play as a large group with one string and kids taking turns blowing, or you can play in teams with two or more strings. The player blowing the cone isn't allowed to touch it with his or her hands. Make sure the kids who hold the string also get a chance to blow a cone.

Game Over

Debrief the game activity.

Work on the temple was sometimes discouraging. It even stopped for 16 years. When you get discouraged, you may feel like you got the wind knocked out of you, and it's hard to keep going. If you feel that way, remember God is in control.

- **What kinds of things make you feel discouraged?** *(not doing well on a test, fighting with a friend, getting in trouble with my parents, being lonely, etc.)*

- **What do you do to stop feeling discouraged?** *(talk with a friend, talk to God about it, listen to music, talk with my parents, read the Bible, etc.)*

- **If you really believe that God is in control, how can that help when you feel discouraged?** *(It can help me look up. I can quit worrying and trust Him.)*

Cooperation Relay

Scripture:
Ezra 7:6-10, 21-28

Memory Verse:
Always give yourselves fully
to the work of the Lord,
because you know that your labor
in the Lord is not in vain.
1 Corinthians 15:58

Bible Background

Just as God had used one king of Babylon (Nebuchadnezzar) to discipline His people by taking them into captivity, He also used foreign kings to allow His people to return. The Book of Ezra recounts three separate returns from captivity in Babylon.

God had prompted King Cyrus of Persia to begin building a temple in Jerusalem and allowed many of God's people to return to Jerusalem. He arranged for the people to take freewill offerings and brought out the captured temple furnishings for the people to take with them. Under his successor, Xerxes, local people opposed the returned Jews when Zerubbabel refused their offer to help rebuild the temple. The story of Esther takes place during this time.

Years later another king, Artaxerxes, also decreed that any who wanted to could return to Judah. Again an offering was taken. The king gave 100 talents of silver from his own treasury. He also provided wheat and wine. He told Ezra to buy sacrifice animals with the offering money. The king commanded that special vessels be taken for use in the temple worship at Jerusalem. He also made it unlawful to require taxes from the Jewish priesthood who served in the Jerusalem temple. Then the king instructed Ezra to teach the people God's law in their land. God used Artaxerxes, a Gentile king, to accomplish His plans.

God doesn't use only famous or important people to accomplish His plans. Think about David, Esther, Jonah, and the twelve disciples—not one important person in the bunch. God loves to use the unknown and the weak because then He gets all the glory. We all have at least one talent or gift from God and God plans for us to use what we have in His service. Remember God can use anyone to accomplish His great plans—even you!

Teacher Tips

- If you prefer, make this activity less competitive and more cooperative by involving several kids in providing instructions to the blindfolded scooper. Have the scooper accompany the runner around the chair so the runner has to guide the scooper as well as balance the peanuts.

- With a small class, don't worry about teams. Even if you only have three or four kids, they will enjoy trying to master the task. If you want to add a challenge, have the group play several times and try to reduce the time the task takes each attempt.

- With a large class, you might want to station helpers to monitor the cups as kids fill them. Monitors can decide when the cup is full enough for the runner to go.

Pre-Game Warm-Up

- Ahead of time, fill buckets with equal amounts of packing peanuts. Plan on one bucket for each five or six kids, with a minimum of two buckets for two teams.

- Give each team a paddle, an empty bucket, two cups, and a paper grocery bag or blindfold.

- Place a chair across the room from each team.

Gear List

- Table tennis paddles or racquetball rackets
- Buckets
- Large disposable cups
- Paper grocery bags or blindfolds
- Chairs
- Packing peanuts

Let's Play!

The Jews who moved back to Jerusalem had a lot of work to do to rebuild the city. It took some coordination and determination. Our game today reminds us of that. Everybody had a job to do. Explain how to play the game.

The first player on each team is the runner. The runner puts one cup on the paddle. The second player is the scooper and wears the blindfold or a paper grocery bag over his or her head. The scooper uses another cup to scoop packing peanuts and tries to pour them into the cup on the paddle. The runner's job is to position the paddle to catch the packing peanuts and to tell the scooper when to pour or when to stop. The cup on the paddle must be full before the scooper can stop. The runner may not touch the scooper or the scooper's cup.

Once the cup on the paddle is full, the runner runs around the chair at the other side of the room without touching the cup, and returns to dump the cup and the packing peanuts back in the bucket. While the runner is running, the scooper puts the blindfold on the next person in line. The old scooper then retrieves the cup from the bucket and becomes the new runner. The third person in line becomes the new scooper. Keep going until everyone has been the runner. The team that finishes first wins.

Game Over

Debrief the game activity.

Everybody in Jerusalem had to pitch in and work together to rebuild the city. They had to look out for each other just the way you did during the game. God used Ezra and He used Artaxerxes who wasn't even Jewish. God can use anyone to accomplish His plans!

- **Describe some ways you worked together to be successful in the game.** *(Answers will vary.)*

- **Can you name another circumstance when everyone had to work together to accomplish something?** *(play a game, tug-of-war, group project at school, etc.)*

- **What are some ways you can see that God might want to use you?** *(Answers will vary.)*

Can You Take the Heat?

Scripture:
Daniel 3

Memory Verse:
The LORD your God is with you,
he is mighty to save.
He will take great delight in you,
he will quiet you with his love,
he will rejoice over you
with singing.
Zephaniah 3:17

Bible Background

Nebuchadnezzar was sure no god could save Shadrach, Meshach, and Abednego from the furnace. He was certain his own gods were superior and they would certainly not rescue three men who had insulted them! Yet one wonders why, after acknowledging God's great power in enabling Daniel to interpret a dream just a few years earlier, he would discount God's power now.

In that seeming acknowledgment of God, Nebuchadnezzar had only complimented the One who had answered his current need, then added Him to a long list of deities. As with many ancient peoples, the Babylonians had a habit of adopting the gods of neighbors and conquered peoples.

The statue is described as gold. It may have been made of a less valuable substance, such as wood, and coated with gold. Daniel 3:4, 7 suggest that the whole population attended the ceremony, but verse 2 makes it clear that the attendees were government employees. Shadrach, Meshach, and Abednego were among them; when Daniel was promoted to ruler of all Babylon, he requested that his friends become administrators of the province (Dan. 2:49). Daniel was their boss. So why wasn't Daniel arrested with them? He apparently was not required to attend. Note that his position, as identified in Chapter 2, is not listed in Daniel 3:2. His job kept him at the royal court in the city (2:49); the statue, at the plain of Dura, was outside the city.

Shadrach, Meshach, and Abednego were rescued from the fiery furnace by God Himself. They may not have known how God would rescue them, but they chose to trust Him regardless of the outcome.

How many times have you faced trials in your life and wondered where God was in the midst of it? Or you may have thought that if you followed God faithfully, you would be spared trials. In fact, the Word promises us just the opposite. But we have Jesus' promise to reassure us: "I have told you these things, so that in me you may have peace. In this world you will have trouble. But take heart! I have overcome the world" (John 16:33).

Teacher Tips

■ For an extra colorful furnace, use red or orange electrician's tape to mark off the boundaries. Throw loose crepe paper streamers inside the furnace.

■ To make the game less competitive and more cooperative, don't emphasize the need to be the first team to finish. Or, play as a large group with only one player in the furnace at a time. While one person tosses the ring, everyone else can be on their knees praying.

■ Play in three groups, with three rings. Have each group represent Shadrach, Meshach, or Abednego.

Pre-Game Warm-Up

■ Ahead of time, inflate rings. Wrap each ring in red, yellow or orange crepe paper streamers. Leave the ends of some streamers loose to look like flames of fire. Tie a 20-foot section of rope to each ring of fire.

■ Use the masking tape to mark off a furnace area about 10 feet square.

Gear List

- 20 feet of nylon or heavy rope for each team

- 2 inflatable swimming rings

- Red, yellow or orange crepe paper streamers

- Masking tape or red or orange electrician's tape

Let's Play!

Shadrach, Meshach, and Abednego didn't care what might happen to them. They believed God would save them, but even if He didn't, they would only worship the one true God. We're going to run into the furnace to remind us what these three guys were willing to do for their faith.

Assign the kids to two teams and have them stand on opposite sides of the furnace. Give each team a ring. At your signal, the first player on each team runs into the middle of the furnace and calls out, "Save me!" The second player on each team tosses the team's ring to the player in the furnace. The first player must catch the ring before it hits the ground and put it on. If this happens, the second player can gently pull on the rope to bring the first player out of the furnace to safety. Then the second player runs into the furnace and the third player tosses the ring. Play continues until everyone has had a turn in the furnace.

If the player in the furnace doesn't catch the ring, the player outside pulls the ring out and tries again.

Game Over

Debrief the game activity.

Shadrach, Meshach and Abednego knew they were in some serious danger, but they trusted God. In the same way, you can trust God too! Our God is able to save us even when no one else can.

- How did you feel when you were waiting to catch the ring or when you missed? *(nervous, excited, anxious, etc.)*

- Think what it would be like if you really were in danger. How could this story help you know what to do? *(Answers will vary.)*

- Our God can save us! Describe some situations where you can depend on God to save you. *(Answers will vary.)*

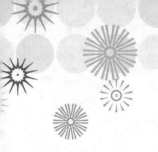

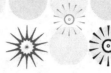

Count On Prayer

Scripture:
Daniel 6

Memory Verse:
Devote yourselves to prayer,
being watchful and thankful.
Colossians 4:2

Bible Background

In this well-known story about Daniel, Babylon is
ruled by Darius (duh-REYE-us). There is debate
about whether this was actually the governor put
in charge of Babylon by Cyrus or if the name refers to Cyrus himself. By this time some of the
exiled Jews had decided to take advantage of the benevolence of the Persian rule and return
home to Jerusalem.

Daniel, now an old man, was not among the returnees. He had built a good career in the civil
service under the Babylonian kings, at times winning their favor and even praise for his God. The
new Persian rulers apparently kept some of the bureaucratic personnel in place, as Daniel
retained his job in the new regime. However, this dependable and honorable ruler still had to deal
with officials who were jealous of his position and power. Once again they used the character of
one of God's servants as a way to get that servant in trouble with the king. Since Daniel was too
good a government worker to be caught in any wrongdoing, they resorted to eliminating him on
the basis of his prayer life.

Many Christians feel they don't pray long enough or often enough. We may think because God
didn't answer our last major request, maybe we just aren't in tune with Him. We may pray when a
need arises, but forget to pray when all seems to be going well. All of this causes many of us to
walk around feeling guilty when prayer is mentioned. If we remember that prayer is a privilege,
an opportunity to come before God and be in communion with Him, that sense of duty will
diminish.

Teacher Tips

- For variety, call out different instructions for passing the beans with each turn—to the left, to the right, across the table, and so on.

- If you're concerned that working with toothpicks will be too difficult for kids in your group, try using craft sticks instead.

- For an extra challenge, see if kids can use toothpicks or craft sticks like chopsticks and pick up a bean with only one hand.

Pre Game Warm-Up

- None needed.

Gear List

- Bowls
- Dried beans
- Toothpicks or craft sticks

Let's Play!

Daniel never stopped praying, no matter what. He must have had a long list of things to pray about! Let's make our own list of things to pray about as we pass prayer beans around the table. We'll pass the beans to remind us that we can support each other in prayer.

Have players sit around a table and give each player a bowl containing an equal number of beans in each bowl. Give each student two toothpicks. Ask kids to take turns calling out something to pray for. This can be family members, pets, schoolwork, friends, sickness, community or world events—anything that comes to their minds. Affirm that we can pray about anything.

After each prayer request, challenge kids to use the toothpicks or craft sticks to pick up a bean and transfer it to the bowl of the person next to them. This way everyone should always have the same number of beans.

Game Over

Debrief the game activity.

No matter what we're praying about, God cares. Praying regularly, the way Daniel did, keeps us close to God.

- **What's your favorite time of day to pray?** *(Answers will vary.)*

- **Where's your favorite place to pray?** *(Answers will vary.)*

- **Name three things you can do to develop a regular habit of prayer.** *(Answers will vary.)*

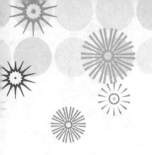

Down with Idols

Scripture:
Amos 2:6-7, 10-12; 5:6-8,
12-15, 21-24; 7:10-15

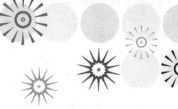

Memory Verse:
Hate evil, love good.
Amos 5:15

Bible Background

Amos was from Tekoa, a small town about six miles from Bethlehem and eleven miles from Jerusalem. He raised sheep and tended a sycamore-fig grove. At God's command he preached to the northern kingdom, Israel, probably mostly at Bethel. Bethel was Israel's main religious sanctuary where the upper class of the northern kingdom worshiped.

When Amos arrived on the scene, he found that not only were the people neglecting God, but they were also ignoring the usual Hebrew ideals of decency and honesty.

The Israelites thought they were righteous, but their actions betrayed their hearts. They offered sacrifices, but they also accepted bribes, hurt those who did right, perverted justice, and sold innocent people into slavery.

High interest rates had forced many Israelites into debt. Some of the poorest families found themselves bound into actual slavery for their debts. Sexual immorality and drunkenness were rampant. In the marketplace, customers were overcharged by tradesmen who had become so greedy for profit that they could hardly wait for religious days to be over so they could go back to making more money.

Amos's message was a call to repentance. He pointed out the people's sins and encouraged them to return to the Lord. He encouraged them to hate evil and love good—deceptively simple, right? But how do we do this?

When we feel overwhelmed with the needs and evil around us, what can we do to help? We can let the love of Jesus shine through our actions and words. We can speak out for the oppressed and hurting. We can pray for God's help and wisdom and strength.

Teacher Tips

- Adjust the distance between the tossing line and the sculpture according to the age and ability of your kids.

- To replay the game, have the kids cooperatively rebuild the idol and then take turns knocking it down again. Each time, challenge them to build a sculpture that represents something different.

- Plastic containers also work well for stacking and building. If you use plastic, you might want to use beanbags rather than foam balls for the extra weight.

Pre-Game Warm-Up

- None needed.

Gear List

- Empty boxes and cardboard containers, taped closed
- Masking tape
- Beanbags or small foam balls

Let's Play!

Aim for groups of five to seven kids to play this game. With large numbers, plan on two or more sets of supplies so groups can play simultaneously.

The Israelites thought they were living the good life! Things were going really well—people started to forget that they needed God. Other things became more important.

What is an idol? *(Anything that becomes more important to us than God is.)* **In some religions, people build or make statues or sculptures of the things they worship, such as animals, spirits, or even people. But an idol can also be something that has value to a person and keeps them from giving God their first love and worship.** Review some of the activities from the Bible story that people allowed to become more important than God.

To play the game, have each group stack up the boxes into a large shape or sculpture. The sculpture can represent a religious idol from Old Testament days or an abstract concept of what became more important to the people than God.

Use masking tape to mark a line on the floor a distance from the "idol." One by one, players take turns standing behind the line and tossing one or two beanbags or foam balls at the idol to knock it down. When the whole idol has fallen, the group celebrates by jumping up and down and shouting, "There is only one God!"

Game Over

Debrief the game activity.

Amos was a shepherd, but God gave him a different kind of job to do. He helped the people remember the things that please God and start doing them again.

- **When you see something wrong happening, what can you do?** *(offer to help, point out a better way, stick up for someone, get an adult, etc.)*

- **What kinds of things do people today make more important than God?** *(love money, possessions, families, themselves, etc.)*

- **How can we keep from falling into the trap of making something more important than God?** *(keep our focus on Him, spend time praying and reading the Bible, ask friends and family to help, etc.)*

Tied Up in Knots

Scripture:
Jonah 1—4

Memory Verse:
Love your neighbor
as yourself.
Matthew 22:39

Bible Background

Nineveh was the chief city of the Assyrian Empire, and generally known as a "great" or large city. Of Israel's oppressors, none were crueler than the Assyrians. To discourage their captives from revolting, the Assyrians brutally punished them wherever they met resistance.

Jonah spent three days and nights inside a great fish. The New Testament clearly uses Jonah's experience as a foreshadowing of Jesus' time in the tomb (Matt. 12:40). As a true prophet of God, Jonah could and did speak of judgment and forgiveness to Israel, but he wasn't ready to accept God's compassion for others outside of Israel—especially the hated Assyrians.

Incidentally, the word "whale" isn't mentioned in the book of Jonah, nor was there a word in Hebrew that specifically translates "whale." The writer used another word that could have been translated "shark" or "sea creature."

Because the book of Jonah is so different in form from the other prophetic books, some have called it a parable. The message of the book, however, would not be changed if it were a God-inspired parable instead of a historical account. The Bible gives no hint that it is a parable. A contemporary of Amos, Jonah himself is mentioned in 2 Kings 14:25, and Jesus referred to him as a real prophet who preached to the Ninevites (Matt. 12:39-41).

God told Jonah that despite the Ninevites' evil ways, He was concerned about them. God wanted Jonah to be concerned as well. Unlike Jonah, we probably don't have to travel to a distant country to find people we don't really like. While many of us have a sense that we should like everyone, realistically most of us have people in our lives that grate on our nerves or whom we simply avoid because of their manner, speech, or behavior. If you are struggling in this area, ask God to help you see him or her as someone God loves.

Teacher Tips

■ To vary the game, set a higher minimum length for each "rope," such as five or six players rather than three.

■ Consider having anyone who has been Jonah sit out so that it becomes harder and harder to escape the tag of each new Jonah.

■ Position Jonah in a central spot in the room and make a rule that Jonah must be standing in that spot when calling out directions. This prevents Jonah from getting too close to one player before calling "rope breaks."

Pre-Game Warm-Up

■ None needed.

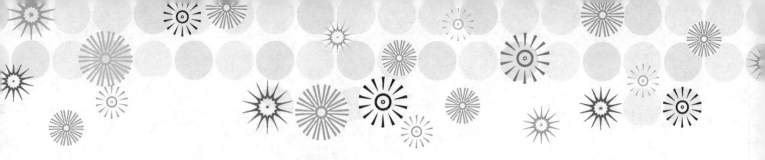

Gear List

- Optional: Signs that say "Nineveh" and "Tarshish"

Let's Play!

Jonah was tied up in knots about what God asked him to do! He was at the end of his rope! The last thing he wanted to do was go to Nineveh. But if he didn't go, then he would be disobeying God, and that was bad, too. It seemed like there was nothing in between.

Before beginning the game, point out two zones on opposite sides of the room that represent Nineveh and Tarshish. If you're using the optional signs, affix each one to a wall or another stable item.

Choose a player to be "Jonah." **Jonah will show us his inner anguish by calling out commands that the rest of you have to obey.** Explain the directions to all the players.

"Make a rope" means the kids will hold hands to make one or more "ropes" of at least three people—the longer the better. The first person in each rope must be touching either Nineveh or Tarshish. This is the first direction Jonah should call out.

"Tie a knot" means the last person in each rope must go under the arms of another pair in the same rope while still holding hands. If there are more than three kids in a rope, they will tie more than one knot.

Other instructions to call include: "untie the knot," "swing the rope," "roll up the rope," "unroll the rope," "make a loop," and "switch ends." These directions are self-explanatory, but you may want to go over an acceptable action for each direction before beginning. The first person in the rope can't let go of Nineveh or Tarshish.

"Rope breaks" means all must let go and run to the opposite zone. Players attached to Nineveh must run to Tarshish. Players attached to Tarshish must run to Nineveh. Jonah tries to tag someone. The first person tagged is the new Jonah and calls out, "Make a rope" to begin a new game.

Game Over

Debrief the game activity.

Jonah had some serious lessons to learn. He had a tough time with obedience. Sometimes God wants us to do things we don't really want to do. But just like Jonah, we need to learn to care about people that God cares about, even if we don't like them.

- **What had Jonah tied up in knots?** *(God told him to go to Nineveh, and he didn't want to go. He didn't like the Ninevites.)*

- **What kinds of things tie you up in knots?** *(having to do something I don't want to do, tests, meeting new people, etc.)*

- **What lesson can you learn from Jonah's story?** *(God wants us to care about everyone because He loves everyone.)*

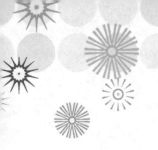
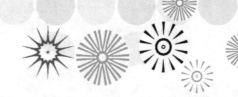

Penny Pick-up

Scripture:

John 4:43–54

Memory Verse:

Come to me, all you who are
weary and burdened,
and I will give you rest.
Matthew 11:28

Bible Background

He went to Galilee. The Galileans' talk of Jesus'
miracles and signs might have given an official of
Herod's hope that Jesus would heal his son.

Unlike the centurion who told Jesus to say the word and his servant would be healed (Luke 7:1–10; Matt. 8:5–13), the royal official might have thought Jesus had to travel to his son. While Jesus marveled at the centurion's faith, Jesus took the official's shaky faith and made it stronger.

Jesus' words in John 4:48 weren't directed at the royal official, but at the unbelieving crowd. But the official took Jesus' words to heart and begged Him to help his son. When Jesus said, "Your son will live," He wasn't predicting a long-range happy ending to the story. He spoke the word, and 16 miles a way a boy was restored to health.

Back at the royal official's house, anxious servants must have noticed the remarkable recovery. Filled with joy, they could hardly wait for their master's return. The servants' joy and their eagerness to meet their master say a lot about the ideal relationship they had with the official. When the royal official asked about the time of the healing, his faith in Jesus' word was confirmed by experience. He and his household believed in Jesus, and believing in Jesus, the Son of God, is the aim of John's gospel (see John 20:31).

The official learned that he could trust Jesus to help his family. So can we. Whether we are just stretched beyond our capabilities or struggling with major issues such as fractured relationships, serious illnesses, divorce or death, Jesus is here to help our families too.

Teacher Tips

- Encourage kids to pair up with someone other than their best friends.

- If you think kids will try to make the task easy by dumping the pennies carefully in a neat pile, make a rule that says they have to swish their hands through the pile three times before beginning to pick them up.

- Have the kids help clean up. Ask them to count pennies to make sure they've picked up all of them and aren't leaving any on the floor.

Pre-Game Warm-Up

- Ahead of time, put 30 pennies in each sandwich bag. Prepare one bag for each pair of kids you expect.

Gear List

- Pennies
- Sandwich bags
- Blindfolds

Let's Play!

Have kids pair up. Blindfold one member of each pair. This player should also put one hand in a pocket or behind his or her back. Give each pair of students a bag of pennies.

When I give the signal, the person in your group who isn't blindfolded will dump the pennies out of the bag onto the floor. Then the person who is blindfolded will pick the pennies up and put them back in the bag—with one hand. The seeing partner may hold the bag open, but the bag must stay in one place. The seeing partner may also give verbal directions to the blindfolded player about where to find pennies.

When all the pairs have finished, switch roles so everyone has a chance to pick up the pennies.

Game Over

Debrief the game activity.

In the Bible story, the royal official must take Jesus at His word when He promises to heal the official's son from a long distance. Sometimes it's hard to trust when we can't see clearly what is happening. We have to learn to depend on Jesus to help us in ways we cannot help ourselves.

- **Tell about a time when you had trouble trusting another person.**
  (Answers will vary.) Be prepared to share from your own life as well.

- **Tell about a time when you may have had trouble trusting God.**
  (Answers will vary.)

- **What are some things would you like to trust Jesus for in your family?**
  (Answers will vary.)

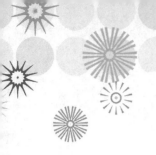

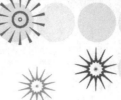

Turnaround Hop

Scripture:
Acts 9:6, 20-31; 13:1-4

Memory Verse:
Offer your bodies as living sacrifices, holy and pleasing to God—this is your spiritual act of worship.

Romans 12:1

Bible Background

Before he came to know the Lord Jesus, Saul was very active in the persecution of Christians. His conversion must have been quite a shock for his Jewish friends and the Christians who had feared him. At that time, certainly no one could have any idea how dramatic the change in Saul's life would be.

Luke tells us in Acts that Saul immediately began to preach to fellow Jews in Damascus. When Saul began preaching, he was met with much skepticism—even from Christians. Those he had persecuted weren't initially convinced of his change, but they came to understand that the power of his teaching could have only come from one source—God. Doubting Christians were won over, and Saul was on his way to fulfilling God's plan. Saul also must have needed time for quiet thought, so he withdrew to the desert of Arabia. Evidently, he spent many months spending time with God and studying His Word (Gal. 1:15-17).

When Saul returned to Damascus to preach in the synagogues, his words touched people in a way that could have only come from God. However, there was still opposition, and some people plotted to kill him, forcing him to flee from Damascus to Jerusalem.

Once Saul was in Jerusalem, the Christians were still cautious, but Barnabas trusted Saul. Later, Saul and Barnabas followed God's call and served together as missionaries. Paul's life after his encounter with Jesus was certainly different.

How is your life different from before you knew Christ? If you came to know Jesus at an early age, this may be difficult to pinpoint. However, the continual work of the Holy Spirit is to make us more like Jesus: "But when he, the Spirit of truth, comes, he will guide you into all truth" (John 16:13). The differences in our lives should be a result of the inner changes that God is making in us.

Teacher Tips

- Extend this game by challenging the kids to carry the balls to the box in a variety of ways, such as tucked under the chin, wedged between the head and shoulder, hopping backward, and so on.

- You can play this game as an individual challenge or a team relay.

- Make sure the boxes are low enough that kids can drop a ball in from their knees, but for extra challenge make them high enough to make the task slightly difficult.

- You may want to station an assistant near the boxes to make sure kids call out a new way to live before retrieving the ball and running back to the start line.

Pre-Game Warm-Up

- Write on blank sheets of paper the phrase "New Ways." Tape a sheet to each box.

- Prepare one box for every six or eight students.

- Use the masking tape to mark off starting lines across the room from the boxes.

Gear List

- Boxes, medium-size, low cut, one per team
- Rubber balls, one per team
- Blank paper
- Marker
- Masking tape

Let's Play!

Paul's life turned inside out and upside down. After he met Jesus, he believed things he never thought were true before. Now Paul did everything differently. We're going to do a few things differently ourselves.

Divide the kids into two teams and line them up behind the start lines. Give the first player on each team a rubber ball. **Put the ball between your knees. When I say "go," hop down to the box with the ball between your knees. Here's the catch: We want to remember that Paul's life was turned around by his new ways. So as you hop, spin in circles at the same time. When you jump up to hop, twist so that you land facing another direction.**

Drop the ball into the box. What does the box say? *(New Ways.)* **After you drop the ball in the box, call out a new way that you can do something to bring glory to God. Then you pick up the ball, run back to your team and give it to the next player.**

Game Over

Debrief the game activity.

After Paul's life turned around, he preached a new message: God calls Christians to do things differently.

■ **Tell about a time you learned to do something in a new way.** *(Answers will vary.)*

■ **Name some ways Christians are different from people who don't believe in Jesus.** *(they love people, are nice, don't swear, etc.)*

■ **What are some new ways would you like to learn to serve God?** *(Answers will vary.)*

Two Get the Job Done

Scripture:

Acts 14

Memory Verse:

Now it is God who makes both us and you stand firm in Christ.
2 Corinthians 1:21

Bible Background

Paul is proof of the fact that the life of a believer isn't always easy. Throughout his entire preaching career, Paul and his companions were harassed, threatened, beaten, and imprisoned. These hardships, however, didn't deter Paul from following Christ and taking His message through the known world.

Acts 14 begins with Paul preaching in Iconium. Many believed his teachings, but others were angered by his words and threatened to kill him. This persecution forced Paul to flee to Lystra. In Lystra, however, radical Jews caught up with Paul and stoned him, dragged him from the city, and left him for dead. By God's grace, Paul recovered and was able to preach the next day.

Paul's next stop was the fast-growing church of Antioch. It was here that Barnabas originally had recruited Paul (Acts 11:25–26). These two men traveled through much of the known world, preaching God's Word. Many people were saved, but others were still hostile to the message of Christ, so Paul and Barnabas were harassed and threatened.

After the lame man of Lystra was healed, the inhabitants thought Paul and Barnabas were gods and tried to make sacrifices to the missionaries. In refusing their sacrifices, Paul and Barnabas may have offended the people of the city, making them more receptive to incoming persecutors. Throughout this time God was with Paul, keeping him safe. No matter how dangerous or scary the situation, Paul did what he knew God wanted him to do.

Today persecution may be more subtle than that which Paul faced. You may have someone who harasses you about being a Christian or who shuns you because you shared your faith. Anytime we live our lives for Jesus, we risk persecution. But remember God will give us the strength and courage to stand firm.

Teacher Tips

- Depending on how many kids you have, you may want to set up several stations with tubs of water and plastic balls.

- To keep slips and spills to a minimum, place the buckets of water on a couple of beach towels.

- As another option, use buckets of sand and marbles instead of water and plastic balls.

- If you want to add an extra challenge, play a second round. In the first round, let everyone get used to the tasks. In the second round, keep track of how quickly the pairs accomplish the tasks.

- As a reminder that Paul and Barnabas faced difficulties as they traveled around, put up signs of names of cities from the Bible story. Place "Iconium" at the start line. Hang "Lystra" over the buckets of water and "Antioch" over the finish line.

Pre-Game Warm-Up

- Ahead of time, place the buckets on the beach towels and fill with water or sand. Toss in a few balls or marbles depending on which option you are using. Set a ladle or slotted spoon near each bucket.

- Use the masking tape to mark start and finish lines across the room from each other. Place the buckets in between the start and finish lines.

Gear List

- Blindfolds
- Buckets or tubs
- Beach towels
- Water or sand
- Plastic or table tennis balls or marbles
- Ladles or large slotted spoons
- Masking tape

Let's Play!

Paul and Barnabas teamed up to get the job done! They traveled from place to place telling the good news of Jesus. When they ran into trouble, they encouraged each other. Let's do a couple of things to remind us that although following Christ can sometimes be tough, having someone to help makes things easier.

Explain the challenges. Kids will work in pairs, like Paul and Barnabas. At the start line (Iconium), one person will put on a blindfold. The pair moves to the buckets of water (Lystra) and the blindfolded player picks up a ladle. The goal is to scoop out three balls from the water. The partner who can see may give instructions. After finding three balls, drop them back in the bucket. Finish by moving together to the finish line (Antioch.) Remove the blindfold, and run back to the start line. Then switch jobs. Each player has to scoop out three balls.

Then each pair should move on to the final task, representing how Paul and Barnabas moved on to a new city. Have pairs stand back-to-back and link arms at the elbows. Connected this way, they must walk from the start line to the finish line and back again.

Game Over

Debrief the game activity.

Following Christ can be tough. Paul found that out when he was beaten and put in prison or chased out of town. But he kept moving and telling people about Jesus.

- Name something you've done to follow Christ that was harder than you thought it would be. *(Answers will vary.)*

- What are some ways you have or may experience persecution for following Jesus? *(getting called names, being laughed at, people not wanting to be my friend, etc.)*

- What's an important lesson we can learn from the way Paul followed Christ? *(to keep trusting Him no matter what, etc.)*

Better Together

Scripture:
Acts 18:1-23

Memory Verse:
If anyone serves, he should do it with the strength God provides, so that in all things God may be praised through Jesus Christ.
1 Peter 4:11

Bible Background

In Corinth many Jews resisted Paul's message, so he began reaching out to the Gentiles, which was a turning point in his ministry. Paul's frustration with unbelieving Jews is evident in his outburst in Acts 18:6. No doubt he was tired of their resistance in city after city. It seems that Paul's turning to the Gentiles caused a change of heart in some of the Jews. It was then that the synagogue leader named Crispus believed. Many more turned to Jesus as Messiah; they believed and were baptized.

God's promise to Paul in Acts 18:10 is similar to the promise He made to His disciples in Matthew 28:20, "Surely I am with you always." The promise was specific and unique to Paul's situation, but the principle applies to all of us.

How good it must have seemed to Paul to work with less opposition in Corinth! After being jailed at Philippi, driven out of Thessalonica and Berea, and laughed out of Athens, he now settled down for many months of work in Corinth.

Paul was able to do a great deal of teaching in Corinth, but eventually he aroused the anger of some Jews there. Their court case before Gallio backfired. Gallio eventually gave Paul and other Christians permission to teach all they wanted about Jesus.

Could Paul have done all this work without God's help? Not only did he rely on God's help, he also needed His encouragement. As you read Acts 18:9-10, note that Paul may have been thinking he couldn't possibly do the job God had given him. God promised to be with Paul. In the same way, He is with you and will help you.

Teacher Tips

- If players seem to be at a stalemate when it comes to progressing toward one circle, encourage kids to think creatively about how to achieve the goal. For instance, one player might pull back and let the other player take control of the ball to get it in a circle. Then the pair can work together to move the ball to the second circle.

- You might prefer to give players a time limit for how long they can try to get the ball into a circle. Even if they don't succeed, their turn is over and it's time to move on to the next pair.

- If you're working with a large group of kids, you might want to have more than three circles, or two sets of three circles in different areas of the room.

Pre-Game Warm-Up

- In advance, use the masking tape to make two or three plate-sized circles on the a table. Label the circles A, B and C. Use masking tape to mark an "X" in a spot that is approximately equal distance from each of the circles. This will be the starting point.

- Also write A, B, and C on the slips of paper and put them in a basket or bowl. You'll need enough slips of paper for each player to have one. You can repeat the letters as many times as necessary to make enough slips.

Gear List

- Table tennis balls
- Masking tape
- Slips of paper
- Basket or bowl
- Pen

Let's Play!

Have kids pair up for this game. If you have an odd number of kids, you can have a group of three. Each player should draw a slip of paper from the basket or bowl and look at it without letting his or her partner see what's on the slip.

Paul preached to different groups of people. Some of them listened to him, and some of them didn't. It might have been hard to tell if he was making any progress! That's what our game is like. The goal in this game is to blow this ball into the circle matching the letter you just drew. You've got to work with your partner to blow the ball into your circle, but don't tell your partner which circle you're working toward. Each of you will be working toward the letter you drew.

Let the first pair try the activity. Have them get down on all fours and place the ball on the X. Obviously, if they both drew the same letter, they'll quickly blow the ball into the appropriate circle. Otherwise, they'll be working against each other. Don't comment on this, just let partners have fun trying to get the ball into their circles. Then let another pair or trio have a turn.

Once everyone has had a turn, time pairs and compare the time it takes when they choose the circle ahead of time and can work together.

Game Over

Debrief the game activity.

Today's story was about Paul and some other Christians who were better together because they were working together and knew that God was with them. Their hope in Jesus gave them a bond, and they could serve each other and other people better because they were working together as a team.

- When was it easy for you to get the ball into your goal? *(when we were blowing toward the same circle)* When was it hard? *(when we were working toward different circles)*

- Name some situations where we sometimes forget that God is working with us. *(in difficult times, when we get hurt, when people harass us, etc.)*

- If you really believe that God helps you with everything you do, how would that change how you feel about some hard things? *(they wouldn't seem so hard, I wouldn't complain as much, etc.)*

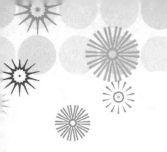

Trust Steps

Scripture:

Acts 20:22–23; 21:1–15

Memory Verse:

We know that in all things God works for the good of those who love him, who have been called according to his purpose.

Romans 8:28

Bible Background

Against the advice of nearly all his friends and companions, Paul set out for Jerusalem. Although Paul knew traveling to Jerusalem would bring hardship, he was convinced that he had to go there and complete the work God had given him.

Friends from several churches accompanied Paul on his trip from the Greek cities to Jerusalem. Luke joined the group at Philippi and later described the journey in some detail in Acts 21 and 22.

It's important to realize that Paul didn't go to Jerusalem against the Holy Spirit's leading, but because of it. Paul's friends pleaded with him not to go because of the dangers that awaited Paul there. Although the Holy Spirit had warned Paul about hardships and difficulties, that didn't stop him.

On the way to Jerusalem, Paul made several stops to visit old friends and fellow believers. He stayed with Philip on one of these stops. Philip's evangelistic work may have focused on Caesarea for almost 25 years. Philip's daughters may have been dedicated in a special way to serving the Lord. At another stop, a prophet named Agabus warned Paul again about going to Jerusalem. This is the same prophet who had been in Antioch prophesying the coming famine in Jerusalem about 14 years earlier (Acts 11:27–29). Despite the warnings of Agabus and others, Paul was willing to totally trust God even if it meant hardship or death.

Have you faced circumstances when it was hard to trust God regardless of what the outcome may be? When we think of trusting Jesus, it is usually the present and the future we are trusting Him for. But when we look at our pasts, all Christians can remember times and events in which we've trusted God and in which He has faithfully kept us and did not let us down. We can be certain that if God has helped us before, we can trust Him with all our tomorrows as well.

Teacher Tips

- Make extra snowshoes in case some are damaged during play.

- Help the kids tie on the snowshoes, threading the strings under their own shoelaces or shoe straps before tying them securely.

- To walk, kids need to pick their feet up only slightly and take sliding steps forward. Although in real snow they would not need to slide as much, this will keep the snowshoe box from folding under their feet.

- For a challenge, appoint a timekeeper and see how long it takes for everyone to complete the loop of stations. Or, keep time on individuals. If you choose this option, you might want monitors to be sure kids fully complete the task at each station.

Pre-Game Warm-Up

- Make cardboard snowshoes for the kids to use during this game. For one snowshoe, cut off and discard the side panels and top flaps of a large cereal box. Leave the front panel, bottom, and back panel in one continuous piece. Open this piece and trim the large rectangle to make a snowshoe shape with rounded edges. Punch two holes on each side, two inches from the edge and in front and behind the center creases (box bottom). Thread two pieces of heavy string, 2½ feet long, through the holes and across the bottom of the snowshoe for laces. Plan on making one pair of snowshoes for every four or five kids.

- Next, prepare five construction paper signs with a large number on the front and directions written on the back, as follows:
  1—Get dressed for snowshoeing. Put on one winter item.
  2—Toss 20 "snowballs" in the bucket.
  3—Continue to station 4. Sing a praise song as you go.
  4—Be careful! Narrow path!
  5—Time to stretch. Do five toe touches and five heel touches. Then go back where you started.

- Place the signs around the room so they create a clear path to follow. At Station 1, put gloves, mittens, winter hats, or scarves. At Station 2, place a bucket and some newspaper "snowballs." At Station 4, mark a narrow path, about two feet wide. Use yardsticks, tape, ropes, or other objects.

Gear List

- Large cereal boxes, two for each pair of snowshoes
- Scissors
- Heavy string
- Construction paper
- Markers
- Winter gloves, mittens, hats, and scarves
- Newspaper, wadded up
- Bucket
- Boundary markers like yardsticks, tape, rope
- Hole punch

Let's Play!

Paul knew that he didn't have an easy road ahead of him. Going to Jerusalem was dangerous, because Jewish leaders there wanted him out of the way—permanently. But Paul knew God wanted him to go to Jerusalem, and he trusted God. We're going to put ourselves into Paul's shoes and go where God leads, even if it's hard.

Have several kids put on the snowshoes you've prepared ahead of time. Send the first player to Station 1 to follow directions there. When that player moves on, start the second player. As players finish all five stations and return to the starting point, keep feeding kids into the trek.

Game Over

Debrief the game activity.

Paul probably didn't wear snowshoes and throw snowballs on his trip to Jerusalem, but he did make some stops along the way. He trusted God at every step of his journey.

- **Tell me some situations where Paul might have been tempted not to trust God.** *(when he was persecuted, jailed, beaten, etc.)*

- **Tell me some situations where you may be tempted not to trust God.** *(when I feel alone, when I'm being teased, etc.)*

- **Tell me about a time when you trusted God and you're glad you did.** *(Answers will vary.)*

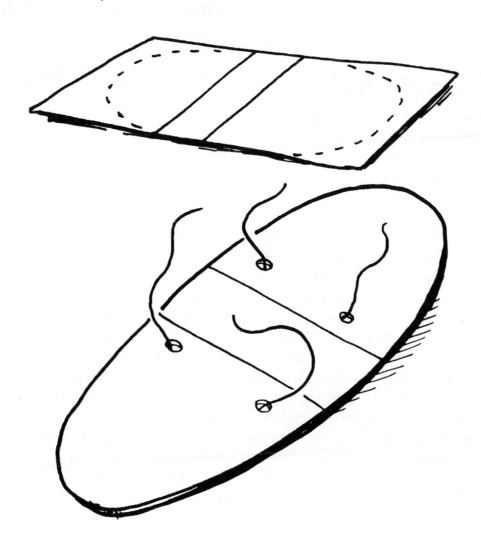

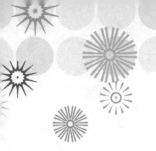

Step by Step

Scripture:
Acts 25:13—26:32

Memory Verse:
At that time you will be given what to say, for it will not be you speaking, but the Spirit of your Father speaking through you.
Matthew 10:19-20

Bible Background

Festus, governor of Judea, had a prisoner, Paul, who had appealed to Caesar, but there were no reasonable charges against him. Fortunately for Festus, King Agrippa came along.

Herod Agrippa II was the last of the Herods. When he showed an interest in meeting and hearing this Paul about whom he had heard, Festus was relieved. Festus was hoping that with Agrippa's help he might better understand the conflict between Paul and his fellow Jews.

As a Herodian, King Agrippa was fiercely loyal to Rome and had no qualms about turning against a Jew. King Agrippa also knew the Old Testament Scriptures and could follow Paul's argument. Festus, on the other hand, apparently knew little of Jewish history or religion. His accusation that Paul was crazy betrayed this lack of knowledge. His outburst was unexpected since Paul was addressing Agrippa. But Festus couldn't understand all Paul was explaining, especially about Christ's resurrection as well as the resurrection of the dead in general.

Paul's challenge to Agrippa to admit that he believed in the prophets may have embarrassed Agrippa. Even if he had been considering Paul's claim, he couldn't let Festus know that. So his response about becoming a Christian was likely sarcastic.

When the opportunity arose, Paul was ready to share what Jesus had done for him, and God helped him do it. Sharing our faith with others may seem intimidating, but just as in Paul's time, people today will be more ready to listen when we share what Jesus has done for us. God will help us as we speak out for Him with the Good News.

Teacher Tips

■ You might want to mark a start and finish line for each team to be sure players don't stop stepping on the cardboard too soon.

■ For a more cooperative and less competitive version of this activity, give each team four pieces of cardboard. Form teams of five or six kids. The rule would be that every player on the team has to be standing on cardboard at all times. How will they get to the other end?

■ If desired, this game can be played outside in a larger open space. Use cones as markers for the start and end lines.

Pre-Game Warm-Up

■ None needed.

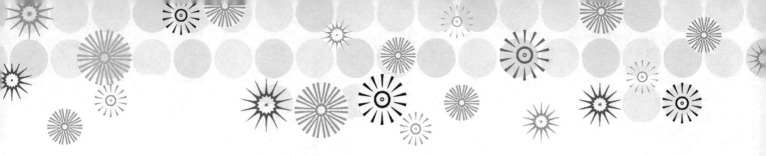

Gear List

- Two or four sturdy sheets of cardboard per team

- Cones for markers (optional)

Let's Play!

Paul was in prison, but that didn't keep him from speaking up. Sometimes we feel like we're in prison and can't speak up. It's almost as if our hearts and minds are behind bars. This story about Paul reminds us that we don't have to feel trapped when it comes to talking about Jesus.

It can be difficult to take that first step in speaking out against something wrong or harmful. It's hard to be different from the group. But if we take that first step, we can set an example for other kids around us. If those kids see us speaking out for Jesus, maybe they'll take that first step too.

Assign the students to two relay teams and have the teams stand at one end of the room. Give the first player on each team two sheets of cardboard. Tell the players that to complete the relay, they must use the cardboard as stepping-stones.

The first player on each team stands on one sheet of cardboard at the starting line in front of his or her team. At a signal, these players must place the second sheet of cardboard out in front of them. They must then step to the second piece of cardboard, reach back, pick up the first cardboard, and place it in front of them. The players should continue this process until they reach the designated finish line. Then each player picks up the cardboard pieces and quickly walks back to the starting line to tag the next player in line. (For extended play, or if the room is small, you can also let the players follow the stepping-stone process to return to the starting line.)

The next player follows the same procedure and continues the relay. The relay ends when all the players have returned to their original places in line.

Game Over

Debrief the game activity.

    Paul didn't always know what would happen next, but he trusted God day by day and looked for every chance he could find to tell someone about Jesus. Speaking out for what's right is easier if we go step by step, a few words at a time.

- **How can we help each other speak up about Jesus without getting nervous?** *(trust God, pray about it, practice with our friends who are believers, etc.)*

- **If you could tell someone three things about Jesus, what would you say?** *(that He died for them, that He loves them, that He wants a relationship with them, etc.)*

- **Name some people in your life who have helped you know Jesus better.** *(Answers will vary.)*

Cooperation Challenge

Scripture:
2 Corinthians 8—9

Memory Verse:
Therefore, as we have opportunity, let us do good to all people, especially to those who belong to the family of believers.
Galatians 6:10

Bible Background

The spirit of cooperative giving was evident in the early church. In Jerusalem, the first believers sold their possessions and shared with others to meet needs (Acts 4:34-37). The church in Antioch took an offering for the poor believers in Jerusalem (Acts 11:27-30). Paul was one of those who delivered the gift.

The famine mentioned in Acts 11 may have contributed to the poverty of the Jerusalem Christians. Another possible factor includes persecution, which may have caused Christian business owners to suffer loss because of their faith. Finally, the Jerusalem church may have had to support or provide hospitality to many Christian teachers who would have come to visit and meet in Jerusalem.

As Paul established churches around the Mediterranean, he taught them to join in giving to the Jerusalem believers. His plan was to have each church take up a collection, then he would revisit their churches to gather the gifts and take them to Jerusalem. That would give the churches time to take the collection. Like the other churches involved, Corinth was a Gentile church, but the believers who would receive their gifts were Jewish.

The generosity of the Gentile believers was also remarkable because they, too, were not wealthy. They suffered under the heavy taxation of Roman rule. Yet they wanted to give, and they gave beyond their apparent means.

Paul's instruction and the example of the early churches provide a challenge to all of us as we seek how we should give. True giving is not about external actions—it is a willing response of the heart that comes from the gratitude we feel for all God has done for us. Share this with your students as they play today's game.

Teacher Tips

- Make the path as long and winding as your space will allow. To make things more interesting, consider whether you can go outside your usual classroom, even just down a hallway.

- If you don't have long ropes, masking tape is another way to mark off a path. At the end of the activity, have kids help you pull up the tape and discard it.

- Encourage each pair to find a new way to hold the ball between them, rather than copy the first successful strategy they see.

Pre-Game Warm-Up

- Ahead of time, use the ropes or masking tape to mark off a long path on the floor, one rope or length of tape on either side of the path. Make the path wind back and forth across the room. Inflate the beach balls.

Gear List

- Beach balls
- Long ropes, jump ropes, or masking tape

Let's Play!

Jesus wants you to show love to your families and others, the way the early Christians showed love by being generous with each other. This game is a fun way to practice showing love by working together to accomplish something.

Have kids pair up and select several pairs to play first. Give each active pair an inflated beach ball. **You and your partner have to find a way to hold the ball between you without using your hands. See if you can follow the path together without dropping the ball.**

Have one pair start down the path. When they're about a third of the way through, start another pair. As pairs finish the path, keep feeding new pairs into the starting point.

If a pair drops their ball, everyone along the path must stop and let the partners recover their ball and continue before the other pairs can move.

Game Over

Debrief the game activity.

One way of showing love is being generous and cooperative. In other words, we show love when we think about other people, not just ourselves.

- **How did it feel to work together to accomplish something?** *(good, fun, satisfying, etc.)*

- **What are some ways that you could cooperate better at home? At school? With your friends?** *(Answers will vary.)*

- **When you think about other people, and not just yourself, how does that help other people know Jesus better?** *(it shows what He is like, they see Jesus' love, they may be willing to listen to the Gospel, etc.)*

Ready for the Game

Scripture:
2 Timothy 3:10—4:5

Memory Verse:
All Scripture is God-breathed and is useful for teaching, rebuking, correcting and training in righteousness.
2 Timothy 3:16

Bible Background

At the time Paul wrote Timothy, Paul was imprisoned in Rome under the emperor Nero. In his first imprisonment, Paul lived in a rented house. It is believed that Paul then was released for a time. Later, when the persecution of Christians intensified, Paul was arrested again. This time, tradition says, he was kept in an underground dungeon, awaiting execution as a common criminal. Even Paul's friend had a hard time finding out where he was being kept (2 Tim. 1:17).

Paul's letter to Timothy was solemn, but not downhearted. Paul had led Timothy to the Lord and considered Timothy his spiritual son. Paul was giving his final challenge to the young man he had discipled and loved deeply.

Paul knew that Timothy would face persecution and that people would reject his message. Timothy, being from Lystra, had firsthand knowledge about some of Paul's sufferings in that region. Paul visited Antioch, Iconium, and Lystra on his first and second missionary journeys.

Paul exhorted Timothy to remain true to God's eternal Word. Through human authors God has revealed Himself in His Word. By remaining true to that Word, Timothy could be sure he spoke God's truth.

The final charge Paul gave Timothy was to preach the Word "in season and out of season" (2 Tim. 4:2). To preach God's Word confidently, Timothy had to know and be equipped by it.

What do you think of when you picture being "equipped?" God has supplied the ultimate tool to equip us for everything we will face in this life—the Bible. How do we use this tool? Do we let it sit on the shelf between Sundays? Or do we allow it to fully prepare us each day so that we can correctly wield this tool (2 Tim. 2:15)? We desire to be those who are fully equipped and prepared, handling accurately the Word of Truth.

Teacher Tips

- If you can't collect enough brooms for every player, use some creative substitutes for sticks. Some ideas include the cardboard cores of wrapping paper, whiffle bats, yardsticks, newspaper rolled and taped into tube shapes.

- Hold firm to the rule that sticks must be touching the floor at all times! Don't hesitate to remove a player from the game if he or she is blatantly breaking the rule and endangering the safety of others.

- If your playing space is limited, adapt for a less active version of the game without sticks. Have players sit in chairs in rows several feet apart. Ask them to grip the seat of the chair with their hands, then hook one foot behind one leg of the chair. Players are not allowed to use this foot. Everyone plays with one foot and tries to pass the whiffle ball back and forth without losing control.

Pre-Game Warm-Up

- None needed.

Gear List

- Brooms (one per player)
- Whiffle balls
- Large playing space

Let's Play!

Assign players to two teams. Have them form two lines 10 to 20 feet apart. The lines should face each other and space players about three feet apart.

Paul was in prison once again, but once again he is busy encouraging other Christians. He doesn't want the game to end, even if he can't play in person. So he's coaching young Timothy to remember God's Word. He's passing on the torch of ministry to someone else so that the "game"— spreading the Gospel—keeps going.

Distribute a broom or "stick" to each player. Starting at one end of the line, the first player passes the whiffle ball to the person across from him or her. That player passes the whiffle ball back to the second person in the other line. The object is to have players zigzag the ball down the line and back again, making accurate passes to each other. Remind players that the brooms ("hockey sticks") are to touch the floor at all times. If a broom is raised above waist level, it is "high sticking," just as in hockey and is not allowed. The player doing so will be removed from the game.

Begin slowly, but then encourage players to see how quickly they can pass the whiffle ball from one end of the line to the other. Emphasize the importance of getting the whiffle ball directly to each person, while still keeping it under control.

Game Over

Debrief the game activity.

Paul knew his ministry was coming to an end, but he also knew God's ministry would go on forever. Just as we kept the whiffle ball going from side to side, Christians keep the ministry ball going. And just like Paul told Timothy, we need to be equipped, and the only thing that will equip us for life is the Bible.

- **Why do you think Paul felt God's Word was so important?** *(because he knew it would equip Timothy for the work ahead, he had already tested it and knew he could rely on what it says, etc.)*

- **How does the Bible help us live our lives every day?** *(Answers will vary.)*

- **Share something the Bible says that you think would help the rest of us.** *(Answers will vary.)*

Topic Index

Scripture Index

Bible-in-Life Correlation Chart

Title	Page	Scripture Reference	David C Cook LifeLinks to God New Life College Press Reformation Press Wesley Anglican	Echoes The Cross
Where, Oh Where, Has the New King Gone?	18	1 Samuel 8—10	Unit 25, Lesson 1	Unit 25, Lesson 1
Battle-Line Stomp	22	1 Samuel 17	Unit 25, Lesson 3	Unit 25, Lesson 3
Friends, Friends Everywhere	26	1 Samuel 20	Unit 25, Lesson 5	Unit 25, Lesson 5
Share and Share Alike	30	1 Samuel 30:1-25	Unit 26, Lesson 7	Unit 26, Lesson 7
Sneak Attack	34	2 Samuel 14:25—15:37; 17—18;	Unit 26, Lesson 9	Unit 26, Lesson 9
Take Aim and Serve	38	1 Kings 4—10	Unit 27, Lesson 11	Unit 27, Lesson 11
Dangerous Quicksand	42	1 Kings 11—12	Unit 27, Lesson 13	Unit 27, Lesson 13
Turnaround Hop	82	Acts 9:6, 20-31; 13:1-4	Unit 28, Lesson 2	Unit 28, Lesson 2
Two Get the Job Done	86	Acts 14	Unit 28, Lesson 4	Unit 28, Lesson 4
Better Together	90	Acts 18:1-23	Unit 29, Lesson 6	Unit 29, Lesson 6
Trust Steps	94	Acts 20:22-23; 21:1-15	Unit 29, Lesson 8	Unit 29, Lesson 8
Step by Step	98	Acts 25:13—26:32	Unit 30, Lesson 10	Unit 30, Lesson 10
Ready for the Game	106	2 Timothy 3:10—4:5	Unit 30, Lesson 12	Unit 30, Lesson 12
As Close as It Gets	46	1 Kings 18	Unit 31, Lesson 1	Unit 31, Lesson 1
Double Whammy	50	2 Kings 2:1-15	Unit 31, Lesson 3	Unit 31, Lesson 3
Tied Up in Knots	74	Jonah 1—4	Unit 32, Lesson 5	Unit 32, Lesson 5
Down with Idols	70	Amos 2:6-7, 10-12; 5:6-8, 12-15, 21-24; 7:10-15	Unit 32, Lesson 7	Unit 32, Lesson 7
Cooperation Relay	58	Ezra 7:6-10, 21-28	Unit 33, Lesson 9	Unit 33, Lesson 9
Can You Take the Heat?	62	Daniel 3	Unit 33, Lesson 11	Unit 33, Lesson 11
Count On Prayer	66	Daniel 6	Unit 33, Lesson 13	Unit 34, Lesson 13
Prayer Catchers	14	1 Samuel 1:1—2:21	Unit 34, Lesson 2	Unit 34, Lesson 2
Keep On Moving	54	Ezra 1—6	Unit 34, Lesson 4	Unit 34, Lesson 4
Sheep Sharing	6	Genesis 13	Unit 35, Lesson 6	Unit 35, Lesson 6
Penny Pick-up	78	John 4:43-54	Unit 35, Lesson 8	Unit 35, Lesson 9
Faith Targets	10	Exodus 11—12; 29:15-18; John 1:29	Unit 36, Lesson 10	Unit 36, Lesson 10
Cooperation Challenge	102	2 Corinthians 8—9	Unit 36, Lesson 12	Unit 36, Lesson 13